# YOUR PETS' SECRET LIVES

## The Truth behind Your Pets' Wildest Behaviors

Eleanor Spicer Rice, PhD
illustrated by Rob Wilson

≡ mit Kids Press

For the cats, dogs, hamsters, mice, snakes, spiders, insects, hermit crabs, birds, squirrels, lizards, turtles, fish, rabbits, newts, worms, and unidentifiable creatures who have made their home with me. And for my parents, Jamesie and Kathryn, and my husband, Greg, who let them all in.

ESR

For my parents and grandparents, who always warmly welcomed the vast array of pets I loved into our lives, hearts, and home. That is, all except for that one bull snake I found (it had to stay outside).

RW

Text copyright © 2024 by Eleanor Spicer Rice, PhD
Illustrations copyright © 2024 by Rob Wilson

The MIT Press, the ☰mit Kids Press colophon, and MIT Kids Press are trademarks of The MIT Press, a department of the Massachusetts Institute of Technology, and used under license from The MIT Press. The colophon and MIT Kids Press are registered in the US Patent and Trademark Office.

First edition 2024

Library of Congress Catalog Card Number pending
ISBN 978-1-5362-2647-8

24 25 26 27 28 29 CCP 10 9 8 7 6 5 4 3 2 1

Printed in Shenzhen, Guangdong, China

This book was typeset in Youbee.
The illustrations were done in pen and colored digitally.

MIT Kids Press
an imprint of Candlewick Press
99 Dover Street
Somerville, Massachusetts 02144

mitkidspress.com
candlewick.com

# Contents

# Introduction

More than half of us live with at least one creature that is not a human. Though they may have scales, fins, fur, or feathers, we consider them family members. Sometimes they might even  seem like humans. Many greet us when we come home; some give us kisses or try to make us feel better when we're blue. But trust us: our pets see the world in a totally different way than we do.

Our lovable housemates have superpowers that come from their ancestors' wilderness survival skills. Some battle ancient foes, if only in their minds. Others can change color or shape. Still others have conversations that we can't see or even hear.

These behaviors seem mysterious, but if you pay attention and know what to look for, you will begin to understand your pet in a whole new way. In these pages, we unlock some of our pets' strangest behaviors. We shake their family trees, peek between their feathers, dive into their brains, and sometimes hitch a ride on their poops to uncover their hidden lives and reveal them to you.

What you do with these discoveries is up to you. Will you give your cat kisses with your eyeballs? Listen to your mouse's roars? Comfort your tarantula when she has nightmares? Congratulate your dog on a well-aimed pee? Give your goldfish some happy memories to last a lifetime?

You know your pets better than anyone. And soon, after reading about their secret worlds, you may be able to understand them, too.

Part I

# Dogs

Of course, you and your pup are best buds! You
do everything together! Well, almost everything.
There are some things a dog just needs to do
on its own. Like poop in the most spectacularly
secret way. And send you tail-wag flag signals.
And . . . turn the page to find out!

# Talk to the Tail

Sometimes we say it best when we say nothing at all. With that in mind, here's a short list of some of the many everyday ways we talk with our hands instead of our mouths:

Wave: *Hello.*

Shrug: *I don't know!*

Raised hand: *Hooray!*
or *I'm over here!*

Shrug: *I'm not really
feeling it.*

Prayer hands: *Bless
your little pea-pickin' heart.*
or *Thank you.*

Punch fist: *You dirty rascal!*
or *I'm gonna beat you up!*

Power fist: *We are the
champions, my friend.*

Peace sign: *Peace out,
homeslice!*

There are plenty more, of course. Some you're probably not allowed to do. Don't do those!

Dogs can talk without talking, too. Their paws don't allow for much in the way of a thumbs-up, so they let their tails do the talking instead. Are you listening to those wags? If you are, you can learn more than just who's a happy pup.

Here is a short list of everyday posterior postures to help you decode the tail talk.

Tail up: *Hello! You have my attention!*

Circle wag: *You are my very favorite of all the favorites, and I am so happy to see you in the most wonderful of ways!*

Wag to left: *You make me nervous, and I'm not super sure about you.*

Wag to right: *I want to make you my buddy.* or *I'm very happy to see you, buddy!*

Tucked tail: *Yikes!*

Also tucked tail: *Come and get me, sucker!*

Yes, a dog's tail can be a window into its sunny little soul. Some tail positions are practical. Tucking that tail in, for example, makes it harder for anyone to nab Buster, whether he's skittering off in play or worried someone's going to bite him. A perky, upright tail can leave the back door open for a good old-fashioned butt sniff.

Scientists think dogs' brain wiring leads to other tail positions. In dogs (and other animals, like humans—like YOU!), each side of the brain specializes in a different set of skills and feelings. The right side of the brain controls the left side of the body and links to using energy (run away!). It also links to feeling sad or afraid. The left side of the brain controls the right side of the body and links to feel-good, happy, calm-type feelings.

When a dog like Buster sees another dog wagging its tail to the left, Buster's heart starts pounding. He acts anxious. Even without knowing everything the scientists know, Buster somehow associates

that other dog's left wag with the feeling that something is a little iffy about the situation.

On the other hand, when Buster sees another dog wagging its tail to the right, his heart rate stays nice and easy. He feels free to wiggle-waggle on up to that dog. With that right-tail-wag signal, Buster feels glad to see an old Buster buddy, or hopeful to make a new one.

Keep your eyes peeled for the silent signals from your best friend's rear end. Is your buddy ready for fun? Or needing comfort? Now that you can catch the meaning of the wag, you'll know for sure.

# True North, Poo North

Have you ever watched your dogs go to the bathroom? It's a whole process. They get all official and serious. They sniff here and snuff there. They turn their bodies this way and that. Right around the time you're about to scream, "JUST GO, BARNABY!" they lift, squat, or hunch with a look on their faces like they're doing the most important job in the world. For what it's worth, it is a Very Important Job.

Dogs tell each other A LOT when they go to the bathroom. Barnaby can sniff a whiff of another dog's pee and tell the dog's age, whether it's male or female, and whether it's open to becoming the future Mrs. Barnaby and making lots of little Barnabys to cheer the world with their velvety ears and hearts of gold. Barnaby can also tell whether or not there's a new dog in town.

Your dog might even be able to tell how big another dog is by sniffing to see how high its pee goes. When Brutus Maximus (who is a very large dog) pees on a stop sign, his pee falls from a great height. When Butch (who is a very small dog with a big-dog name) pees on the same stop sign, he can't get his leg high enough to match Brutus Maximus's giant pee stain.

Peewee males like Butch might try to mask their shorty status. When they go number one, they lift their legs as high as they possibly can to aim the stream. Researchers watched big dogs and little dogs pee on stuff. (A related point: The world is full of amazing job possibilities, like watching dogs pee. You can do whatever you dream of doing!) These researchers found that when little male dogs pee, they not only stretch their legs up high; they also turn as far as they can to the side to really shoot that pee for the stars. Aim high, little guy!

Butch might be trying to pretend he's a giant, or he might be trying to cover as much of Brutus Maximus's pee with Butch pee as he can. Either way, dreaming big and peeing high can send a major message.

That's only the beginning of K-9 bathroom superpowers. Dogs also have an amazing hidden talent that reveals itself when they go to the bathroom. If the world is calm and all things are equal (no hurricanes, no electrical solar storms, no owner yanking at the leash saying, "Come ON, Ms. Pertookins!"), dogs (male *and* female, whether they like to aim high or not) turn their bodies to align with the north–south axis of the earth's

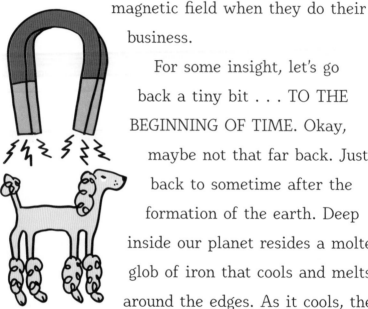

magnetic field when they do their business.

For some insight, let's go back a tiny bit . . . TO THE BEGINNING OF TIME. Okay, maybe not that far back. Just back to sometime after the formation of the earth. Deep inside our planet resides a molten glob of iron that cools and melts around the edges. As it cools, the glob creates electrical currents. These currents make up a magnetic field that stretches from the earth's center to outer space like a force field.

This magnetic-field-generating system is called the geodynamo (JEE-oh-DIE-nuh-moh).

The magnetic field is super handy. Be glad we have it. First, it battles solar winds, those charged particles that the sun flings in our direction. Solar winds could, and do, disrupt important tools like electricity and navigation 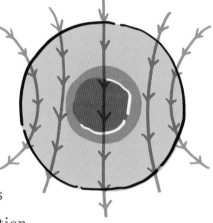 systems, which require charged particles. Have no fear! Our magnetic field is here to deflect them!

Animals use the magnetic field, too, usually to locate home. The field runs roughly in a north–south direction. This means animals that can detect it get their bearings without a map. Though we likely aren't able to detect it ourselves, humans have been using the magnetic field to navigate for thousands of years. The magnetic field is the reason our compasses point north. Sharks and sea turtles use the field to find home. Many songbirds have little proteins in their eyes that help them detect the field so they can track their way around the planet. It's like they have tiny compasses built into their eyeballs.

Back to dogs. It's no secret that dogs are super great at making their way home. In the 1920s, Bobbie the Wonder Dog (who was probably just called Bobbie at the time) got lost in Wolcott, Indiana, when he and his family were on vaca-

tion. He walked 2,551 miles (4,105 kilometers) to reach his human family, who had returned to their home in Silverton, Oregon. To get there, he traveled across places he'd never

been. He probably had a lot
of questions for his family
when he got back and
discovered they'd
gone on home without
him. Bobbie's amazing,
but he's not alone in his

wayfinding abilities. The magnetic field is one
of the most important long-distance navigational
tools for dogs. They reveal this truth when they
go to the bathroom.

For whatever reason (we don't really know
why), many animals like to orient their bodies
in alignment with the earth's north–south
magnetic field. Cows, deer, naked mole rats,
mice, and others seem to feel better when they're
communing with the chill waves of the ole
geodynamo. Think of it the next time you see a
herd of cows hanging out. Which way are they
facing? And dogs, for whatever reason (we don't
really know why), prefer to relieve themselves

when their bodies are lined up the same way. Which leads us to believe that dogs can detect the field. Which leads us to believe that one of the ways dogs find home is by using the earth's magnetic field like a compass. Which reminds us that dogs remain marvelous, even when they're taking a poop.

# Worst-Case Scenario: A Tale of Two Wormies

It was the best of grimes, it was the worst of grimes. It was the age of deliciousness, it was the age of squirms. We're talking about worms, of course. Worms that might live inside your dog. Some pretty horrifying things can happen to your dog (like a tick bite that paralyzes her; plus, she sniffs butts for fun!) on a fairly regular basis. Worms are some of the most horrifying of all.

Although a bunch of different creatures we call worms can steal your dog's heart (literally steal the organ that is your dog's heart, or its intestines, or its skin, or—*shudder*—many other places), two of the most common types of wigglers are tapeworms and heartworms. Each one has its own wacky way of worming into your dog's life. Buckle up for a ride on the worm train.

**Tapeworms**
look kind of like skinny, white, flat ribbons. They grow up to 11 inches  (28 centimeters) long and move in a gentle, fluttering sway. Sound pretty? Their mouths are made of hooks that clamp to your dog's intestinal wall while they sway around in your dog's almost-ejected dookie.

"How did they get there?" you wonder. It wasn't easy.

It all begins in a fresh pile of dog droppings. Or a little before that, deep up a dog's butt. There, an adult tapeworm releases one of its body segments, packed with up to twenty of its eggs. The segment slips into poop as it passes out of the dog and onto the ground. The egg packet looks like a whitish cucumber seed. Because it's a segment of the worm, it can wiggle around on Brown Mountain for a couple of days before it settles down, dries out, and breaks open, releasing its eggs.

Here is where it gets weird, even for butt worms. The eggs wait around for a special someone to eat them. Want to know who that special someone is? No, not your dog. It's a baby flea.

Baby fleas (you can call them larvae if you want) don't resemble smaller versions of grown-up fleas. Instead, they look like slim, hairy maggots, a little shorter than a grain of rice. If there were a cuteness competition for maggots,

 these larvae would win the grand prize.

Flea larvae don't live on animals or slurp pet blood like their parents do. They squiggle around on the floor.

There, they search for random gunk to eat, like the food and dirt and other stuff you ground into the carpet. Or tapeworm eggs.

So this baby flea, who we're going to call Bingo, has a tapeworm egg for breakfast. The tapeworm hatches inside Bingo. It grows up in Bingo's intestines. Yes, Bingo's got worms. Bingo has worms when he pupates. Bingo still has worms when he emerges as a full-grown, dog-hungry flea. Bingo is a grown-up flea, after all, and grown-up fleas eat animal blood for breakfast, lunch, and dinner. That's too bad for

your pup. Because it looks like Bingo just found
your dog and hopped on.

Once he hitches a ride
on your dog, Bingo does
what Bingo does best
and starts squeedling
around your dog's fur.
This is itchy to your dog. She
starts to bite at the itchy spot and nabs Bingo.
She swallows him, worms and all. That's the end
of Bingo, but it's not the end of the worms. They
make their way, along with Bingo's body, through
your dog's digestive tract to her intestines. There,
they burst from Bingo's corpse. They reveal their
hooky mouths and chomp down on the intestinal
wall, settling in for a life of worm making and
poop eating.

Bingo needs your dog, and the worms need
your dog *and* Bingo.

If your dog is a puppy, tapeworms could stunt
her growth or make her sick. The worms eat

the food meant for your puppy. And, for puppies and adult dogs, tapeworms itch like crazy. How do you scratch a butthole itch if you don't have fingers? Why, you hunch down and drag your worm-filled butthole across the carpet, of course. Butthole dragging can be an indication that your dog might have an inner life that's richer than simply dreaming of chasing squirrels through fields of bones and orchards of open peanut butter jars. In fact, your dog's inner life might actually be alive and writhing.

**Heartworms**, on the other hand, need a different creature to make their way into your dog's body: the mosquito. Heartworms can grow even longer than tapeworms—14 inches (36 centimeters). They are super deadly. Adult heartworms live in dog hearts. They can become so abundant (hundreds in one dog!) that they clog the heart and arteries so your dog's organs can't get the blood they need to work. It's awful. They could never have gotten that far without the help of mosquitoes.

What happens is a mosquito named Missy (all mosquitoes that drink blood are female) bites the dog down the street, who has heartworms. Mama heartworms make millions of baby heartworms called microfilaria (MY-kroh-fuh-LER-ee-uh). Baby heartworms like to lurk inside a dog's tiny blood vessels, those closest to the surface of the skin. When Missy slurps dog blood infected with heartworms, all of a sudden she has a problem she doesn't know about. Like our old flea friend Bingo, Missy has worms.

For the next couple of weeks, heartworm babies develop in Missy's guts. They feed on the food she gathers for herself, which is animal blood. When they're ready, the little worms swim up

Missy's body and hang out in her mouth. The next time Missy bites a dog, when she jabs her needlelike mouth into the  dog's skin, she also jabs a mouthful of microfilaria right into the dog's bloodstream.

Those microfilaria swim around the dog's blood. They grow (and grow). In a few months, they collect in the dog's heart to make millions more babies.

Just like how tapeworms need Bingo, heartworms need Missy.

It is a far, far better thing to eat the poo (or squash the mosquito) than to get worms.

# Doggie Howlser, MD

In the early 1990s, Doogie Howser was a bright teenage doctor on television. Sure, some viewers doubted his youth and his unconventional methods. But Doogie was there to heal, and you never doubted his results.

Want to know another unconventional medical practitioner? Your dog! While some of his behaviors may seem strange (grass gobbling, anyone?) and gross (scarfing down at the poop buffet!), there's a method to his madness. Don't hate, congratulate! Doggie Howlser, MD, is in the house. Let's look at some of his patients' files.

**HEALTH CONCERNS:** Unsanitary habitat, possibly leading to butt worms

**PRESCRIPTION AND TREATMENT:** Eat any poop less than two days old.

Translation for humans: Lots of dogs eat poop, and some dogs eat a lot of it. They're only trying to keep things clean, y'all. When her puppies are newborns, a mother dog wolfs down their number twos as fast as she can in an attempt to keep their den clean.

As those babies grow, most of them also eat poop. Under one condition: the poop must be fresh (expiration date: two days). Scientists used to think dogs ate dookie because they were missing some important vitamins in their diets or maybe because feces just tasted good to dogs. Well, maybe they *do* taste good, but after taking a deeper look, researchers found that most dogs eat only fresh poop.

When intestinal worms hit the ground, wrapped in their egg cases, those worms aren't able to infect other dogs until their poopmobiles dry out. This takes a few days. Scientists think one reason dogs eat poop is to get the worms before the worms can get them. That's why dogs scarf dook before the egg cases burst forth with a bounty of butt munchers. Good dog!

**HEALTH CONCERNS:**
Do I have worms? Do I? Is there something coming out of my butt?!? I can't tell!

**PRESCRIPTION AND TREATMENT:** Eat a bunch of grass.

Translation for humans: Sometimes dogs eat grass quickly to help them throw up. Because they can't digest the green stuff, grass is just the kick in the guts they need to get the queasies out. But most dogs eat grass on a daily or weekly basis. They can't feel sick *all the time*, can they? Not likely. Dogs' digestive systems can't break down grass, so it's not a nutrient boost for them. Why keep up with the salad days?

Worms, of course! Many creatures, from cats to chimpanzees, eat grass to help rid themselves of the worms infesting their bodies. For these animals, grass comes out the back end looking the same as it did going in the front. When gobbled grass reaches the intestines, it acts like a net or a bunch of ropes. The grass tangles around the worms and drags them out the back end. Dogs can't feel worms swimming around their insides (you wouldn't be able to, either), so they go on and gorge on the green stuff just in case.

**HEALTH CONCERNS:**
Cuts, scrapes, and other various itches and ouches

**PRESCRIPTION AND TREATMENT:** Slobber early, slobber often.

Translation for humans: You may have noticed that when you pick a scab, your dog comes to lick it. Or that you can sometimes tell your dog has a cut by where she's licking. Dog slobber works as a medicinal ointment. It has stuff called bactericides (bak-TEER-uh-syds) that kill microbes like strep and *E. coli,* which can make us sick. It also contains antibodies that can bust up invader parties, plus a host of other ingredients perfect to save the day. We just hope the wound licking doesn't happen too close to the poop eating. You never know.

# SorryNotSorry— Don't Fall for That Guilty Look

## An Interview with Julie Hecht

Julie Hecht spies on dogs, which is a real job. She is an animal behavior researcher at the City University of New York. She also wrote the *Dog*

*Spies* blog for *Scientific American* magazine. In *Dog Spies*, she listened to other people who spy on dogs and then shared what they do. Thanks to her work, you and I know even more about those wet-nosed wonders that brighten our days.

When Julie's not listening to other pet spies, she's spying on pets herself. Sometimes she blows our minds by carefully watching dogs and cats to decode the meaning behind some of their most adorable—or puzzling—behaviors. Like that time when you came home to find your garbage dragged across your kitchen floor. When you started to yell at your dog, Chip, he looked so sad and guilty, and all you could say was "Aw, Chip. I can't stay mad at you. You feel so bad about this!"

Here's the truth: You've got Chip's "guilty look" all wrong. Chip isn't apologizing for having a party with the trash. Something else is going on. Chip probably does not feel bad about this. Chip probably does not feel guilty. It's all in your head! All of it! Chip is a trash gobbler! That's it!

Don't believe us? Take it from Julie, the dog-spying expert. Here, she spills Chip's secrets (and some of ours, too).

Julie, you know dogs, you love dogs. But why spend your life spying on them?

"I've loved dogs since I was a little kid. As I got older, I was blown away to learn that even though dogs are much-loved members of our families, they are not simply small people, or people trapped in dog bodies.

"Dogs (their scientific name is *Canis familiaris*) are an entirely different species from us humans. They have their own distinct evolutionary history and their own ways of looking at things.

"Dog science excites me because we can ask scientific questions about what dogs know, think, and care about. We can also try to find out why they have such amazing, deep relationships with us. Sometimes we find that dogs are a lot like us, but other times we're really surprised by just how different they are!"

But when Chip ate the trash, he really did feel guilty, right? I mean, he LOOKED so guilty! What is going on with that guilty look?

"The dog's 'guilty look' sure is tricky! If you've lived with a dog, you've probably experienced coming home to find that your dog did something he shouldn't have. Maybe he got into the dog treats, the cat litter, the trash, heck, shredded his own dog bed. You think, 'Why, dog?! WHY?!?!!'

"You look at your dog and know something fishy's going on. Just look at him! Maybe he's shrinking away, avoiding looking at you, or approaching with his head down and tail wagging ever so slightly. This dog knows he did wrong. Guilty as charged.

"Only, that's where you've got it wrong.

"Dogs don't view their past behavior in the same way that we might. The behaviors we think of as part of the guilty look aren't actually saying, 'I know I did wrong. I'm so sorry. Won't do it again.'"

Then what do they actually mean?

"Studies show that dogs often act like this when they're around something that they've been scolded for in the past. Let me explain with this pretend example . . .

"Let's say you want to be sneaky-sneaky. When Chip's not looking, imagine YOU tiptoe into the house and YOU drag out the trash like Chip would have. Then you sneak out of the house and leave Chip home alone with the mess. How do you think Chip's going to behave when you come back? After all, he didn't do anything wrong. It was YOU who had a party with the trash!

"But what's this?! When you come back home, you may see Chip with a guilty look on his face even though he didn't actually drag out the trash this time. Wow.

"This is because dogs like Chip who look 'guilty' aren't apologizing. They're not even trying to say that they know they've done wrong. Instead, here's what dog spies like me found out—dogs respond to how YOU behave. Think about it. Dogs are masters at noticing our every move. On top of that, they desperately want to keep the peace with us. After all, we're their family. So if we get mad or even slightly upset about something, they're going to pick up on that, and they're going to show behaviors—like lowering their head or averting their gaze—to try to keep the peace or even calm someone who's upset. Dog spies like me call these behaviors cohesive or appeasement displays, and dogs use them with us as well as with one another. Instead of demonstrating guilt for what he's done, the dog could be feeling fear or distress."

It seems like getting forgiven every time, even if you haven't done anything wrong, is a pretty sweet strategy. So what's the harm of a sad puppy-dog face?

"One problem with believing in the 'guilty look' is that dog lovers may become frustrated with their pets for the wrong reasons. If they think Chip's behavior means he understands and is apologizing for dragging out the trash, they won't get why he would do it all over again. Feeling extra annoyed, dog owners might scold their dogs in a way that doesn't do any good—and may even cause harm.

"Instead of scolding dogs after the fact and thinking they understand, dog lovers can try to figure out why their dogs did the unwanted thing in the first place. Was the dog bored or scared of being home alone? Should the trash be less accessible? Then, with this information, owners can help their dogs to stop that behavior.

"We have the power to help our dogs succeed! No guilt trip required."

# Part II

# Cats

While you're sleeping, your cat is up to its own cat-tivities. Your cat can't help it! Deep within all cats, primal urges swell and rumble like a coming storm. We followed them down the alleys of their instincts and emerged with some of the oddest information about their everyday lives.

# Home on the Range

There's no getting around it: cats are predators.
They're great at their jobs, too! They kill small
creatures like birds, chipmunks, and insects.
The average house cat, left to roam outside, kills
about four animals a month. Multiply that by
all the other kitties in the neighborhood—and by
the neighborhoods across the world—and cats kill
billions of native animals each year.

In many places we live, outdoor cats have become apex predators. That means they're the top predators on the food chain, with no other natural predators in sight. Lions are apex predators of the savannas. Sharks are apex predators of the oceans. Cats are the apex predators of your block.

So far, scientists have found that cats aren't too picky when it comes to what they'll hunt. Cats easily capture more than 1,000 species of animals, from rabbits and birds to marsupials and mice.

Because they feel a need to hunt, whether or not they're hungry, outdoor cats have a "home range," a territory they use for stalking prey and hanging out with their buddies. Researchers put small tracking collars on house cats and found out that most have a home range of about one city block. Some, though, prefer a little more breathing room. A few cats spread their home ranges over a couple of miles.

Scientists also discovered that male cats and younger cats have bigger home ranges and move around a lot more. Once a cat hits the robust age of eight, it starts sleeping a lot and doesn't travel around so much.

Just because they have a home range doesn't mean they need to eat all the tweet they find. If you're a cat owner, you may already know that if you put a bell on your cat's collar to alert birds, she'll probably figure out how to walk so the bell stays silent. Cats are smart! But so are you! You can get your cat a puffy, bright collar that makes her look like an adorable version of the 1500s diva Queen Elizabeth I. In addition to snazzing up your cat's wardrobe, the collar makes it easier for birds to see her.

Also, feeding your cats meals with a lot of meat can reduce their desire to hunt. "But doesn't all cat food have meat . . . ? Wait . . . WHAT IS IN CAT FOOD?!" That's what we wondered, too. It's kind of hard to tell because cat food is either  can-shaped mush that smells terrible or bags of crunchies that look almost like breakfast cereal.

We checked it out. Plenty of cat foods have all kinds of meats in them, but they have other stuff, too. Like tapioca sometimes. And celery. And soybeans. And grains.

If you have an outdoor cat, you can do your part to save the native creatures in your neighborhood by updating her wardrobe. You can also make sure she's not eating soybeans for supper. If all goes well, you'll keep her closer to your porch—all the better to snuggle with.

# Unleash Your Cat's Inner Lion

## An Interview with Mikel Maria Delgado

You already know this if you've watched your cat lounging in a sunbeam like she's just conquered a gazelle on the savanna. You also know this if your foot has drifted a little too far off the side of the bed in your sleep—and into the clutches of Baron von Spikyclaws. You even know this if you've watched your cat try to murder the laser beam on the floor: she might like to cuddle, but

deep inside, your cat is a wild beast with primal urges. Parts of Fluffy's spirit will always remain untamed. But how can Fluffy ever be happy? She is meant to roam! To hunt! To conquer! And she's trapped in your house! Or in your backyard catio!

Have no fear—Dr. Mikel Maria Delgado is a cat behavior consultant. Mikel has peered into the wild depths of your cat's soul. She emerged with an understanding of how to turn your home into the wilderness Fluffy craves. Now she's here to tell us about it.

First, why did you decide to study and work with cats? Didn't you know that trying to understand a cat's feelings is like trying to hold a rainbow? Impossible! They are sphinxes!

"I didn't really have a plan to work with cats. But ever since I was a young child, I've always been very interested in cats. One day I started volunteering at a local animal shelter. I realized that perhaps I would like a career where I could work with animals, ideally cats! I volunteered so much that the shelter offered me a job working in their Cat Behavior Department."

Domestic cats have very different lives from those of their wild ancestors. How can these differences impact our own cat's mentality?

"Cats can get bored, stressed, or frustrated if we don't give them a safe and stable environment. Although many cats enjoy human attention and cuddles, we often want to handle them more than they want to be handled. If we don't give them enough choice and control in how they interact with us, they can get scared or upset, so it's important to be respectful when they need space."

What are some ways we can help our cats feel happier and more connected to their wild cat drives?

"Cats are natural predators. Even though they live indoors and we feed them, they still have a strong drive to hunt! We can help our cats feel more connected to those hunting instincts by playing with them every day with interactive toys like feather wand teasers.

"We can also feed our cats several small meals each day, much like they would eat if they hunted. I also recommend feeding them some food out of food puzzles."

What's a food puzzle?

"Food puzzles are toys that cats must interact with in order to get food out. Like a ball with a hole in it that they can roll around, or a tray with cups and tunnels that they can fish food out of. That makes them feel like they're hunting!"

That covers hunting, but cats have other wild urges as well. How can we help them with those?

"Right. Cats also have instincts to scratch, so you can get tall, sturdy scratching posts for your cats. This will give them an acceptable place to scratch that is not the back of your couch!

"Cats also love to be up high. If you have a few very tall 'cat trees,' ideally in a sunny window where your cats can sunbathe and watch birds and butterflies, you can fulfill that natural urge for height."

Any more feline instincts we can foster at home?

"Yes! Cats have an instinct to cover their waste. They are also very clean creatures (you've seen how often they bathe themselves!), so it's important to provide them with a few litter boxes that are easy to access. Scoop them out as often as you can.

"Cats are predators, but they can also be prey. That means they're naturally wary, on the lookout for something that might want to eat them. Because of this, it's helpful to give our cats cozy, quiet places, like cocoon-style beds, where they can feel safe or have a little alone time."

How can we tell if we have a happy cat?

"A happy cat is healthy and readily engages in typical cat behaviors, such as eating, drinking, using its litter box, playing, sleeping, and interacting with other members of the household. Happy cats will stretch, groom themselves, purr, and sometimes show attention-seeking behaviors, such as meowing, kneading their paws, or rubbing against you."

Does your research ever surprise you?

"We recently published a study that surprised me. There is a tendency for animals to do what is called contrafreeloading, which means they prefer to work for food (such as pushing a button to get a piece of food) instead of just getting food in a bowl. Many species have shown this behavior, including pigeons, rats, giraffes, and even primates. A very old study suggested that cats were the only species that did NOT contra-freeload. The study was very small and done in a laboratory, and I thought it had some flaws, so I didn't trust its conclusion. We did a study to test contrafreeloading with cats in their homes. Well, sure enough, the cats in our study also did NOT prefer to work for their food! I really thought that in the home and with a food puzzle, cats would enjoy working for food since they naturally hunt for food. I was wrong! I guess what I found out is that no matter how long you have worked with cats, they will still surprise you. There is *always* more to learn."

But you still think food puzzles are a good idea?

"I still recommend people offer food puzzles to their cats, but try a few different types of puzzles, and make sure your cat understands and enjoys the game. It makes sense if you think about it: even though I might prefer to play video games over exercising, exercising is good for me!"

Thanks for helping us tame our wild things, Dr. Delgado. We will still try to keep our toes in the middle of the bed, just in case the untamed beast emerges.

# Blink to Me, My Love

Everyone seems to have something to say about cat personalities. Aloof? Temperamental? Superior? Those who know cats best (those of us who love our cats) know that sometimes, yes, cats can seem like they think they're better than we are. Even so, they remain our snuggle bunnies, our partners in crime, our BFFs. They *understand* us. And we *understand* them. It turns out, in many ways, they really do. And we really do, too.

Humans have lived with pet cats for about the last 10,000 years. You don't live that long with a pet and not learn anything from it. Whether we realize it or not, we've learned a lot from cats. People who own cats can tell whether their cats' purrs are urgent (like the  "FEED ME I AM ACTUALLY STARVING" purr) or just pleasant (like the "YOU CAN FEED ME IF YOU LIKE BECAUSE I LIKE FOOD AND I LOVE YOU, TOO" purr).

Our cats also pay attention to us. They learn those weird names we give them, and they come when we call (if they feel like it). If something seems kind of iffy in the room, like a stranger shows up or a weird box appears that might make an excellent cat spaceship, they look to us, their humans, to see whether we think it's cool to proceed. If they can't find something they're

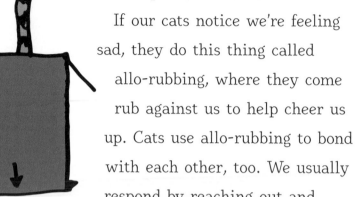

searching for, like a toy, they look to us to help them find it.

If our cats notice we're feeling sad, they do this thing called allo-rubbing, where they come rub against us to help cheer us up. Cats use allo-rubbing to bond with each other, too. We usually respond by reaching out and petting them, or pushing our foreheads against theirs. Got that? They've trained us to pet them, which can boost our moods.

Maybe the most bondy-bondy thing cats have trained us to do is to give them the slow blink. That's where cats slowly narrow their eyes, down, down, and down, as they look at us.

For whatever reason, many of us feel compelled to slowly blink right on back. The slow blink makes cats feel good. It tells them that the world is a safe and calm place, where people take the time to quietly talk to them with their eyes. They have trained us to respond to them in ways they can understand. Because, deep down, we belong to them.

# Catnip and the Cosmic Kitty

Catnip is like, well, catnip to cats. "But what is catnip?" you may ask. "And what does it mean when something is 'like catnip'?" you may continue. "And WHY?" These are all great questions. We're glad you might have asked them. It shows you're thinking. Keep doing that.

Catnip's a plant. Related to mint-type plants, catnip first grew in eastern Europe, parts of Asia, and the Middle East. Today, it grows all over because we humans bring it with us when we move around and plant things. We bring it because our cats love it. They love it because it makes them feel super-duper. Sometimes it makes them feel crazy. Sometimes it makes them sleepy. It always makes them rub things or roll around.  Sometimes it makes them drool. Like, catnip actually takes over their brains and makes them do these things.

Here's what happens. Catnip has this chemical in it called nepetalactone (nep-ut-uh-LAK-tohn),  which we will, from here on out, call Kitty Fantastic Sauce. When catnip leaves are bruised, they release Kitty Fantastic Sauce, an attractant that smells irresistible to cats. You know how when someone's baking chocolate chip cookies in the house and the smell makes you all happy and you feel like you *have* to follow the smell to the kitchen because maybe there are warm cookies there? It's like that, except it's Kitty Fantastic Sauce.

When cats smell it, instead of needing to go to the kitchen to find cookies, they feel like they need to smash their faces on the 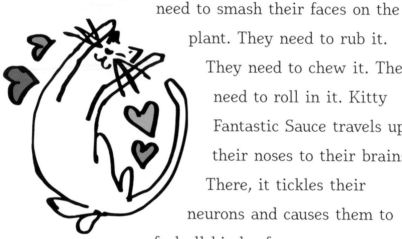 plant. They need to rub it. They need to chew it. They need to roll in it. Kitty Fantastic Sauce travels up their noses to their brains. There, it tickles their neurons and causes them to feel all kinds of awesome.

Cats feel super dreamy from Kitty Fantastic Sauce for about 15 minutes, until their sense of smell gets overloaded. When that happens, cats become "immune" to catnip's alluring effects. But after a half hour or so, their sense of smell recovers. Then they can go wild again, reuniting with their good friend Kitty Fantastic Sauce.

Catnip love is hereditary. While plenty of cats—we're talking lynx, leopards, cougars, and even some lions and tigers— get all googly from Kitty Fantastic Sauce, about a third of cats aren't affected by it at all. Kittens don't seem to care about catnip, either, until they're about six months old.

But those cats who do like to take rides on the Kitty Fantastic Express get an unexpected benefit. It turns out catnip wards off mosquitoes. All that lovey-dovey rubbing is like spraying mosquito repellent all over their bodies. That's a good thing, because in addition to having the primary personality characteristic of being annoying, mosquitoes can transmit diseases, like feline heartworms.

So go on and plant some catnip in a pot, keep it in a sunny spot in your living room, and let the good times roll.

# The Love Loop

When a human parent gazes into their human baby's eyes, something magical happens inside both their bodies. Birthing parents and babies see each other and start to release a hormone called oxytocin (OK-see-TOHS-en). Oxytocin does fantastic things to our feelings. It helps us feel trustful, like we want to help people, like we're not stressed. In general, oxytocin gives us those warm, fuzzy bonding feelings. As the parent and baby are flooded with oxytocin, the feel-good feelings from the baby lead the parent to make feel-good feelings, which leads the baby to feel good about that and make feel-gooder feelings, and so on and so forth until it's a well-established lovefest.

Oh, yes, birthing parents and their babies. Such a deeply human experience . . . Wait . . . except the same thing happens between humans and their dogs and cats. It turns out  that our relationship with dogs and cats is more partnership than ownership. Sure, you are responsible for their food, walks, and health, and for loving them. But they change you—in some ways you can't see.

When you gaze at your furry beastie bestie, it can cause oxytocin to surge in you, and in your pet, and back in you, and back in your pet, until you two are a blissed-out bonded duo.

This happens only with domesticated pets. Stare at a dog that typically lives in the wild, like a wolf, and you might feel something great, but the wolf would just be uncomfortably wondering why you're looking at it. Chimpanzees see your loving gaze as a direct threat! Eyes to the toes, people!

We've been keeping dogs and cats as pets for thousands of years. It's possible this loop of love has helped solidify our BFF bonds. We complete one another.

# Part III

# The Aviary

It's total drama in the birdcage. If the birds aren't
looking for the loves of their lives or hurling
food, they're setting up invisible force fields.
It's time to read between the tweets to find out
what's *really* going on.

# This Flock's Got Talent

Call it a parakeet, call it a budgie, call it
Mr. Wafflebottoms. But please! Call it! Our most
favorite of parrot pets loves calls. Parakeets use
songs to recognize each other, bond with their
buds, and let other birds know that they're
members of the same group.

If you're a male parakeet, learning calls can
make or break your romantic life. Every day for a
male parakeet is like being a contestant in one of

those reality TV talent shows. Except instead of losing out on a record contract or a big fat check, if a male doesn't learn a song and sing it just right, it could cost him his future.

Living in flocks, wild parakeets (and pet para-keets lucky enough to have flocks) spend their days chitchatting. They teach each other sounds and songs. Males can sing more songs than

females, but the females are always listening, always judging. Males need to keep up! That's why, in our homes, they're so good at learning songs and human words. (One parakeet named Puck learned almost 2,000 human words! Let 'em know how you *really* feel, Puck!) See, the ladies want to make sure their boyfriends can learn the right songs in the right ways.

Each female parakeet has her own song that she learned from her parents and buddies. The sounds of that song act like a key to unlock the door of her attention. If a good-lookin' male comes flapping around and shows that he can sort of sing her song right, she might be open to making him her mate. She sings to him, and he sings back to her, trying to copy her tune.

The thing is, once they form a pair, he needs to get her tune exactly right. This is when Miss Judy decides whether her bird boyfriend gets voted off the show. If Mr. Wafflebottoms (that's Judy's boyfriend) is an excellent singer and learns her song just right, the lucky couple is more likely to live happily ever after. They mate and lay eggs and have sweet-singin' chicks together.

What a chipper-chirpy life!

But.

If Mr. Wafflebottoms and Miss Judy form a pair and Mr. Wafflebottoms can't learn her song just right, Miss Judy votes Mr. Wafflebottoms off her singing show. Except she doesn't tell him about her decision. What Judy does instead is secretly listen for other males who sound great. When she finds them, she mates with them before going back to Wafflebottoms. She and

Wafflebottoms have a clutch of eggs, some of which might have been fathered by those other birds. Wafflebottoms works to feed those babies, teaches them the songs he had a hard time learning, and raises them as his own. He never suspects they might be someone else's babies. That's cold, Miss Judy!

It may seem cold, but the truth is, Judy wants her babies to be as healthy as possible. The ability to learn songs well will help them be more successful as adults. By finding the best-crooning mates, she increases the chances that her babies will be good singers, just like their real daddies. Yes, Mr. Wafflebottoms won't be having as many babies that are actually his (sorry, Mr. W), but Judy's babies will contribute to the healthy, bright future of parakeetkind.

# The Secret to a Long, Happy (Bird) Marriage

Cockatiels have it all. First, they win in the looks department. Have you seen them? They're unbelievably cute. Those rosy little cheeks. Those plucky, expressive crests. Those bright, curious eyes.

Second, cockatiels can really sing. Go on, little Chickpea! Sing your heart out, Mr. Yoshi! They have the brains and the pipes to make up songs or sing along with ours.

Oh yeah, and third, they're brilliant. Cockatiels might have tiny brains, but those brains they have are packed with neurons, which make them curious, help them solve problems, and give them a boost when outsmarting other creatures they live with. (Even *you*? Yes, even you.)

But all those looks, tunes, and brains make for one big problem when it comes to finding a mate: If everybody's super awesome, how can anybody find the One?

Imagine yourself going to the best-friends store. There, lining the shelves, are the best kinds of best friends around. All of them can play your favorite sports, video games, secret pretend games, and whatever else you want to play. They can keep you up-to-date on the latest trends and read your favorite books right along with you. And they look pretty similar, too—they have the same amazing clothes. How are you going to find your Very Best Friend Forever out of all these BFFs? What makes one BFF at the best-friends store different from the others?

If you're like cockatiels (and you *are* like cockatiels. We are all like cockatiels. This is good for us. Well, we don't have those crests. And we aren't birds. But in this very important way we are all like cockatiels), it comes down to chemistry. Sure, all those best friends are really great, and it's cool that we have so much in common, but do we even *like* any of them?

In the wild and in our homes, if they're given the chance, cockatiels form long-term relationships. They sort of get bird-married, where they partner up with another cockatiel, settle down, and raise babies together. Just like with people, some couples like each other more than other couples do. Even two cockatiels who are nice-enough birds on their own might find that, for whatever reason, they bring out the worst in each other when they come together.

It turns out that chemistry is the secret to a happy cockatiel home. Bird couples whose partners like each other better are also kinder to

each other. And since they don't fight so much, they have more time to make fertile eggs. They do a good job of coordinating with each other to make sure someone's keeping those eggs incubated. When their eggs hatch, the couples who have the best chemistry are the best parents. Their babies are more likely to grow up to be the independent, well-adjusted, good-looking, brainy musicians we all know and love.

Sometimes, like in our pet shops and cages at home, cockatiels can't choose who lives with them. In those cases, they do the best they can. But when a cockatiel finds true love—the bird they like best in a skyful of delight—they come together to really soar.

# The Man Who Says It's Okay to Be Birdbrained

## An Interview with Melvin Rouse

Dr. Melvin Rouse is an associate professor of psychology at the University of Puget Sound in Tacoma, Washington. Because bird brains are similar to human brains when it comes to some of the ways we learn new information, Dr. Rouse uses pet zebra finches to help figure out how human brains work. Along the way, he makes some remarkable discoveries about bird brains, too. Then he publishes his findings and tells people about them. He shares his discoveries with the whole world! Which means he gets to help each of us (a) love science even more and (b) make more discoveries based on his discoveries, if we want to. Dr. Rouse's research takes a deep look at the inner workings of our gut feelings.

Dr. Rouse gave antibiotics to very young zebra finches and then watched their behavior. If you've ever had strep throat or a sinus infection, you probably know all about antibiotics. We take them sometimes when we're sick, and they work by killing the bacteria that make us feel bad. In the process, the antibiotics can also kill the bacteria that keep our bodies running smoothly. That can have some wacky unintended consequences on our mental and physical health. For example, we know that if we mess with our gut microbiome (all the bacteria, fungi, viruses, and other small creatures that live in our guts), we can become depressed.

Dr. Rouse found that if he gave zebra finches antibiotics when they were young, they acted differently when they were older. He discovered that the zebra finches that had taken antibiotics didn't display as many "affiliative behaviors" as birds that didn't have antibiotics. In other words, they weren't as friendly and outgoing with other zebra finches. The birds who took meds early in life didn't give the kindly "hello!" to other birds as often as unmedicated birds, for example, or they didn't help groom others as readily. Dr. Rouse

and his team think the antibiotics changed the birds' gut microbiomes, which affected their behavior.

In addition to studying songbirds and humans, Dr. Rouse is a songbird himself, a musician who uses nature's musicians to help us understand ourselves. He's here to tell you about how, in some ways, it's cool to be a bird brain.

Why did you choose zebra finches for your study about antibiotics affecting behavior?

"We chose the zebra finch because, unlike humans and some other animals, they grow into adulthood pretty quickly (about six months of age). This means that in a single experiment, we can easily track how the bird grows and develops in response to a specific treatment without having to wait years!"

What's the coolest part of your job?

"My hope is that, one day, a young person will read some of my work and will be inspired, like I was, to become a scientist. I hold on to this hope because back when I was a student, I didn't see many scientists who looked like me or came from a community like mine. So whenever I get to share my work, I think about what that might mean for some young person out there who has never seen a Black scientist in real life and how that young person's perspective is needed to help a global network of scientists make the world a better place for us all."

How did you first get interested in psychology?

"As a young musician, I was fascinated with the process of learning music and was curious about how it all worked in the brain.

"After I graduated from college, I was still curious, and a friend shared with me a really interesting scientific article written by a professor they had had in college. The article was about songbirds and how they learn to sing. After reading it, I was beyond fascinated and just had to reach out to the professor who wrote the article.

"I asked them questions about their research and what they thought it meant about the larger story of evolution, biology, social behavior, and the psychology of learning. We corresponded back and forth for more than a year about science and birds. I made the decision that I not only wanted to do what they did; I wanted to study under them as a graduate student. So began my scientific life with birds and psychology."

We love how you danced to your own beat, Dr. Rouse.

# The Messy Eaters for the Betterment of the World Society

TMEFTBOTWS for short. It's a long name for a club, but anyone who owns a parrot knows they're messy eaters. Not only messy—they're *wasteful* eaters. For anyone who doesn't own a parrot, allow us to tell you: parrots are very smart animals, but when they eat, they look

like they have no regard whatso-
ever for economy. "What is going
on in your little brain?!" you ask
as you watch the parrot take a
small nibble out of a piece of fruit
(parrots love seeds and fruit) and
then toss the rest on the floor and
look at you as if to say, "Pick it up,
my minion." A perfectly good piece of
fruit!

Pet parrots aren't the only parrots
that dump their food all over the
place. Wild parrots do it, too. And
their sloppiness has nothing to do
with whether they're well
fed. They all chomp and
dump like it's their job.
Because it *is* their job. Sort of.

In the wild, parrots live with tons of animals
and plants. Those animals need to eat, and those

plants need to be planted. Researchers who
watched wild parrots eat were just as puzzled as
parrot owners who feel like they spend their lives
waiting with dustpans under their birds' perches.
Both the researchers and the parrot owners were
dumbfounded by the amount of food the birds
hurled to the ground. Food seems hard enough
to come by! Why waste it? Then the researchers
started to look around the parrots.

When they did, they found more than eighty
animal species that ate the food the parrots
dropped from the trees to the ground. They found
hungry ants, other birds, and big wild-cow-type
creatures called zebus. The
researchers saw that not
only did these animals
eat the food the
parrots dropped,
but they also
helped disperse

the seeds by pooping them out with a little fertilizer or by carrying them somewhere else to nibble in peace.

It might not seem to make much sense for the parrot to drop its lunch, but wasteful feeding works wonders for the plants and animals that make up the wild parrot's ecosystem. All that messy eating enriches the parrot's world, which, in turn, makes its life better. More fruit trees to prune. A rain forest full of friends, many looking out for each other.

But what about your kitchen, you say? Time to implement the five-second rule.

# The Canary's Invisible Force Field

Do you have any secret superpowers? Of course you do. You have your microbiome.* You have your sparkling personality, which helps you charm (or repel!) your friends and family. You have pheromones, those chemicals your body puts

---

*Your microbiome is all those invisible creatures, like bacteria and fungi, that live on your body and *in* your body and keep you healthy and alive! You've got one! It's unique to you! Make it count!

out that make other people notice, often without realizing it, that someone they love is nearby, or that you're afraid, or that you're sad.

Look, you have a ton of secret superpowers. You're incredible. You already know that. But we're not supposed to be talking about you right now. We're supposed to be talking about canaries. Those tiny finches with an amazing, giant, invisible superpower.

It hasn't always gone so well for canaries. One minute these birds were bopping around with their buddies in the Azores and the Canary Islands, and the next: BOOM. When European colonizers first encountered them, they stuffed as many as they could in cages and shipped them all the way back home to be pets. Not only pets! No, that

would be too easy. When people realized canaries got woozy from inhaling invisible toxic gases like carbon monoxide, they started putting canaries in boxes and taking them deep into coal mines, hoping the birds would pass out before the people did. When the canaries hit the deck, the people knew they needed to hightail it out of the mine. It worked pretty well for the coal miners. Such heroes! Such dangerous jobs!

To add insult to injury, people started calling criminal tattletales "canaries." They'd say a criminal "sang like a canary" when confessing their crimes or telling on someone else.

We digress.

In the wild, canaries are sociable little birds who flit around in groups with other canaries. As anyone who has been to school knows, groups can be great. You can make friends in groups. Friends are a superpower of their own. Friends can help you solve problems that you might not be able to solve by yourself. They can help you feel happy because you know they've got your back. They're fun to be around most of the time. And friends can also help you defeat enemies you might not be able to defeat yourself. (Not that you have any enemies. We already went over this. You're incredible. But canaries can have enemies. Cats, for example. Or canary-grabbing people.)

As anyone who goes to school also knows, groups can be breeding grounds for diseases like colds and strep throat. One day, a kid shows up looking a little sleepy, and the next day, everyone's got the flu. Diseases can be sneaky like that, hopping from one person to the next.

When canaries, those group-loving songsters, see someone in their group not feeling great, something amazing happens to their bodies. They put up an invisible force field.

Here's what happens.

Like with people, it's noticeable when birds get sick. They can get sleepy-eyed, start moving slowly, and just seem icky in general. If one canary sees another canary with that "I don't feel so good" look in its eye, the healthy canary starts to go on high alert. Healthy canaries watching sick canaries do two things:

1.  Deploy cells called heterophils (HET-uh-ruh-fils) into their bloodstreams. Heterophils act like scrappy soldiers on the lookout for diseases to attack.

2.  Dump bacteria-shredding chemicals called complement molecules from the liver into the bloodstream. These molecules help keep any would-be invaders at bay.

On the outside, the canary looks totally normal. But on the inside, the healthy canary is now cloaked in massive protection, an army of helpers to keep it healthy, even if it has to chill in the same area as Sickeroo.

With their stealthy, invisible-force-field super-powers, canaries may be able to keep hanging out with their buddies while staying as healthy as can be. They don't even need to dump hand sanitizer on their little bird wings and claws or shout, "EW, GROSS! GET AWAY FROM ME!"

As you might imagine, this goes a long way toward maintaining healthy bird friendships, both in the cage and out. Too bad we don't have the same superpower. For now, we'll have to stick with good old-fashioned handwashing.

# Part IV
# The Fish Tank

Your fish tanks hold elephants, matadors, barbarians, and masters of strategy. All you have to do is watch and wait and they'll reveal themselves to you.

# The Guppy's Eeeeeeeevil Eye

Guppies are so small that the name *guppy* is often substituted for *pip-squeak* beyond the fish world. Some guppies max out at about half an inch (13 millimeters) long; the whoppers span about 2½ inches (6 centimeters). They have no stabby fangs, no spines or poisons. To anyone feeling snacky in the tank, guppies are like little swimmy nuggets of deliciousness. Or they would be, except for this: Guppies are brave. And within their tiny fishy skulls, they harbor the power of the Evil Eye—*if* they choose to use it, that is.

You probably know guppies as the eager-looking swimmers in the fish tank. Unlike many other kinds of fish, which lay eggs, a guppy mama gives birth to live young, popping out ready-to-swim, big-eyed babies that the mama will quickly scarf down if she's hungry enough. Oh, don't be so sad about it! Sure, they're cute, but in a month or so, Mama Guppy can pop out more ~~snacks~~ babies. And most guppies in the wild get eaten by *something.* Might as well be Mama!

In the wild, all kinds of creatures eat guppies. To avoid getting eaten, guppies have radical defenses. One defense is being brave. When a weird and potentially deadly fish comes to town, brave guppies swim swim swim around to inspect it to see if it's interested in a guppy buffet. But brave guppies inspect in a brainy way. Instead of swimming up to what scientists call the "attack cone"—or what we call the "mouth"—brave guppies bop around to the back of the predator fish, where it's harder for the fish to eat them.

Other guppies in the guppy group are not so brave. They don't inspect predators. They hide. It turns out that predators largely ignore the guppies that inspect them. They're like, "What's with that joker?" and then they move on to look for something good to eat. Something delicious like a not-so-brave guppy peeking at them through the grass.

Even meek guppies hiding in the grass have their own brand of bravery. If a guppy sees a predator looking at it, the guppy gets really still. Then it does something so outrageous it's brilliant. The guppy turns its head to stare directly at the predator. In a flash, the guppy's eyes change color from silver to jet black. Black, like an abyss. Black, like, "Look at my big, beautiful guppy head. It is right here, and you should come eat it right now."

The predator can't believe its luck. Here is a giant-eyed guppy so easy to eat, stock-still, waiting to become take-out sushi! Is this too good to be true?

It is, Guppyslayer. It's way too good to be true.

Guppyslayer turns to face the guppy. The guppy darkens its eyes more, turning itself into a living bull's-eye. The predator rockets straight for the guppy's head, mouth open, ready for supper. The guppy holds steady, its now giant-seeming eyes lost, pleading. At the last instant, right before you want to cover your own eyes and scream, "Don't do it, Guppyslayer!" the guppy darts to the side. Many types of Guppyslayers can't change direction once they begin charging toward their target, so they're left with a mouthful of nothing.

Lucky for guppies, even the not-so-brave ones have mastered the Eeeeeeeevil Eye, using the Guppyslayers' rocket power against them.

# Oh, Beautiful
# Nanny Barbarian!

Some of us call them betta fish. Others of us
know them as Siamese fighting fish. Still others
call them Mo and Tyrone—whatever you call
them, betta fish males are the orchids of the
fish world.* As they float around the tank, their
fins drift and flow like evening gowns of any
color: red, orange, gold, aqua, royal blue, hot

pink, black, purple, and more. They come spotted like dalmatians, striped like flags, and blooming like the sunrise. So serene, so exquisite, so . . . savage? Beneath their good-looking exteriors, male betta fish have real anger issues—issues humans have bred into them on purpose.

Betta fish (as we most often see them, staring at us from inside fishbowls) are the result of more than 1,000 years of selective breeding. To

---

*Orchids are flowers. They come in all sorts of astonishing shapes and colors. That's how orchids are like bettas. Lots of orchids survive because birds poop on them and the flowers eat that poop as fertilizer. That's one way orchids are not like bettas. Also, some orchids smell good,** and we've never actually sniffed a betta, but we hear they smell sort of fishy, so they're not like most orchids in the smell department, either. Okay, there are plenty of ways that betta fish and orchids are not alike at all. Look, we're just trying to tell you that betta fish are pretty and come in lots of shapes and colors! Forget the rest of that stuff! It's called an analogy! Go ask your English teacher!

**Some other orchid species smell like roadkill. They smell that way to lure in flies, who get pretty excited about the idea of scarfing down dead animals. The flies help pollinate the orchids. As you might have already guessed, these orchids are not popular houseplants.

understand how that works, imagine a guy named Jim who has lots of betta fish, but he likes the

bright blue ones best. Jim chooses two dashing bright blue fish, sets them up in a betta fish motel (a fish tank), and lets them mate. Out of all the babies they make, Jim chooses the brightest blue pair to send to the honeymoon suite at the Betta Motel.

When they have babies, Jim chooses the brightest blue babies to send back to the honeymoon suite to mate with the other bright blue babies in his betta collection. Jim does this over and over until he has a fish tank full of the brightest, bluest bettas. This is how Jim selectively breeds fish.

People selectively breed all kinds of animals and plants. Our pets, strawberries, corns, and yummy chickens have all been selectively bred by humans to give us the creatures and plants we love to love and/or love to eat.

Compared to pet bettas, wild bettas aren't much to look at. They have shorter fins and more muted colors. Though not as flashy, wild bettas are still colorful, especially the males, who like to show off their stuff like miniature bright peacocks in the dark waters.

More than 1,000 years ago, people in Southeast Asia harvested the brightest swimmy-boy fish with the longest fins and mated them with the brightest girl fish. This makes for extra-pretty fish after a while. But pretty has only a little to do with it. See, betta fish males in the wild have two important jobs, and they take those jobs very

seriously. They are the lovers and they are the
nannies. Don't be fooled by the gentle-sounding
job titles. Fish lovering and nannying is serious
business.

First, the lovering. It can be hard to find a
mate in the wild. Fish are small and the waters
are vast. That's why, when a male betta fish finds
a female who might be interested in becoming
his baby mama, he will
fight to the death to
keep her. See,
when it's
time to
mate, he

swims to the water's surface and begins blowing
tiny bubbles, nudging them along so they clump
together. These soft, protective bubbles are his
nest. Bubble nests take time and energy to build.
If another male comes near his nest, that other
guy could wreck the whole thing. That makes
betta daddies grumpy. So male bettas chase and

aggressively bump other males with their bodies
and heads whenever they see them to keep them
away.

Then, after a betta fish male mates with a
female, she lays eggs in his bubble nest and goes
off to live her best life, leaving him with the
kids. He spends his days rushing around, chasing
off would-be egg eaters. If his babies fall out
of the nest, he gathers them in his mouth and
gently shuttles them back
to their bubbles. These
are his babies, and he
does not play around.
Anyone who gets close
will feel the wrath of his
mighty fishy bumps.

Males need to be aggressive,
but too much aggression in the wild can be
deadly. Going around picking fights all the time
is grueling; plus, one day they might pick a fight
with the wrong guy, the guy who could kill them.

So wild betta fish fight only when they need to. That's not the case with pet betta fish, though. Just as people picked the brightest-colored swimmers, they also picked the fightiest of the wild fish and bred them and bred them and bred them until the male fish had real bad tempers. They

did this because betta fish fighting was kind of like human boxing is today. Folks would bring their prizefighter fish to fight to the death against someone else's prizefighter fish. They'd bet money on who would be the champion. The fish flare their luxurious fins to show they're ready to rumble, and they use them to block incoming attacks from other bettas. Someone could make a lot of money if they had the strongest, fightiest, finniest fish.

Here are a few things that researchers have found make pet betta fish males extra angry:

- Other betta fish males
- Looking at themselves in a mirror
- Seeing a fake male floating around as if it's alive
- Seeing a fake male floating around as if it's dead

It must be exhausting being so angry all the time. Actually, betta fish males don't get angry all the time because they mostly live alone. They mostly live alone because they will try to kill any betta fish male that comes even remotely near them. In the wild, the cumbersome, colorful fins and bad attitudes could spell death for a fish, but the fishbowl keeps them out of trouble and lookin' good.

# Your Goldfish Is Watching You

Have you ever heard anyone say, "Oh, silly me. Sometimes I have the memory of a goldfish!" when they forget something? When they say that, they mean that they're forgetful because they believe goldfish can hold information in their watery little brains for only three seconds. Well, if you ever do hear someone say that, you should shout, "You're WRONG! And your insinu-ation is an insult to goldfish everywhere!" You'll be right. Also, you'll be standing up for goldfish, which is a noble cause.

It turns out understanding your goldfish's exceptional memory can make the difference between believing you own a boring bowl bubbler and realizing you're actually harboring an aquatic savant. However, your goldfish's memory can also commune with its ancestral state to turn your fish's children and grandchildren 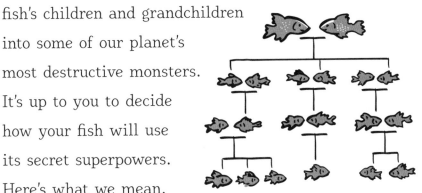 into some of our planet's most destructive monsters. It's up to you to decide how your fish will use its secret superpowers. Here's what we mean.

While goldfish owners everywhere go about their regular lives, most do not realize that Bubbles is watching them from his bowl. Bubbles doesn't forget. And we might not know that packed in his tidy, shimmering body is a beast waiting to be unleashed, a beast that can cause ripples of destruction across vast swaths of the earth. Bubbles does not play around.

Goldfish are a type of carp, which are mostly unglamorous fish that swim along the bottoms of rivers, lakes, and ponds, uprooting water plants and swishing around the sediment as they look for creatures to eat. Unlike their wild cousins, pet goldfish have been bred from wild carp for centu-ries to have shiny, colorful scales and luxurious, floaty fins. Remember bettas? Like that. This means that deep within each goldfish lurks its ancient, wild relative, waiting to be released.

Now, back to that memory. Nobody knows for sure why we think of goldfish as forgetful. Our best guess is that it's because we feel guilty for treating them so badly. Some people (not *you*, of course—you would *never* do this) leave their goldfish in tiny bowls, forget to feed them, and let them swim around in grody-McGroo, poop-filled water. Then, instead of saying to themselves, "Oh, wow. What I have done here to this goldfish is terrible. I should have bought a tank," they say, "Aunt Minnie always says goldfish can't remember anything. Every few moments is a new lifetime to a goldfish! This isn't so bad for ole Bubbles!"

The truth is, goldfish, as far as fish go, are super intelligent. They can remember each other and the different visitors to their bowls. They can be taught to perform tricks, to tell the difference between songs (goldfish have great hearing, BTW), and to navigate complicated mazes. They can remember these things for months or *years*. Yes, years. Because if they're treated well,

goldfish can live up to twenty years. Oh, Bubbles! WHAT HAVE THEY DONE TO YOU?!

Well, it gets worse. Some fish owners decide it's not working out between them and Bubbles. They're faced with a dilemma. On the one hand, nobody wants a secondhand goldfish. On the other, it seems cruel to kill him. So these fish owners dump Bubbles into their local stream. "Bye-bye, Bubbles! You do you!"

The thing is, Bubbles, beneath all his fancy fins, is still a carp. Released from the pressures of a confining bowl and presented with the glorious abundance of the natural world, Bubbles gobbles up all the things he wants from the muck. Bubbles isn't picky. He'll eat fish eggs. He'll eat dragonfly babies. He'll eat pond scum.

The wild world is an all-you-can-eat buffet to Bubbles, and he takes it seriously. In no time flat, he'll grow from the size of a fishbowl resident to the size of the fishbowl itself, or as big as one of your dad's shoes.

Because lots of folks dump their Mr. Bubbleses and Ms. Bubbleses into streams, these fish find plenty of footloose goldfish to mate with. Each goldfish female can lay up to 40,000 eggs a year. Thanks to predators catching the flashier, easier-to-see babies and leaving behind the dull-colored fish (which blend in well with riverbeds), within just a few generations, Bubbles's babies' babies start to look like their ancient ancestors. They drop the delicate-fins-and-shimmering-orange act. Now they are boring browns and yellows, more like the bottom of a pond. This makes them better at hiding. Goldfish can even mate with wild carp and have more carp babies.

These babies and babies' babies are just as hungry as Bubbles. They destroy plants by uprooting them when looking for tiny creatures to eat. They churn up the riverbed as they wallow  around in the depths, which swishes nutritious sediment up toward the surface of the water, fertilizing algae that usually floats harmlessly along. The algae suck up all the nutrients and fill the water with an algal bloom, which can block light and choke out creatures.

Today, goldfish descended from ex-pets are one of the planet's most destructive invasive species. They wreak their fishy havoc on streams, rivers, and ponds, anywhere from Australia to

Alaska. They may be wild, but they still have excellent memories. Recently, people have discovered goldfish banding together to have massive spawning events. Spawning takes place when fish all meet up in a safe spot each year to lay tons of eggs and fertilize those eggs. Released from the endless circling of a fishbowl, goldfish use those brains to achieve their true potential as long-distance swimmers.

Some goldfish migrate more than 100 miles to get to the party, and they keep coming back each year.

Back in the bowl, your own Bubbles swishes his fins, flowy as willows in the wind, as he makes another lap. He recognizes you, and he's waiting for you to play with him. He's ready to show off for you. Recently, researchers trained goldfish to do things even people sometimes find tricky. For example, a group of scientists in Israel taught six goldfish how to drive a little car down the road to pick up

some supper. The car looked like a fish tank on wheels, and the goldfish figured out how to make it move by swimming in the direction they wanted to go. After they got the hang of it, they drove their fishmobile to a target, where a scientist gave them some food. These fish basically learned how to drive cars to fish restaurants to get takeout.

If researchers can train their fish to get takeout, what can you train Bubbles to do? Swim through a hoop? Leap like a dolphin? Fold your laundry? Read *War and Peace*? Join you in your plot for global domination? It's up to you and Bubbles. He's ready.

# Tetras Will Take You to School

Neon tetras look like miniature lasers darting around fish tanks. With their shiny blue stripes and equally shiny red stripes, they turn any swim tank into a rave. They love to swim together in schools. Have you ever wondered why they have such bright stripes? While their stripes make them such good-looking partygoers in your fish tank, in the wild those same stripes give them secret superpowers.

Neon tetras come from Central and South America, and they like to live in blackwater streams. Blackwater is water where plants have decayed and turned the water the color of sweet tea. Some fish have a hard time getting around in the tinted water, but neon tetras use their stripes to help find each other. The males are Straight

Sammies, long and lean, and their stripes look straight. The females have little curved bellies, which make their stripes look bent.

Not only do these shimmery stripes help tetras find one another in the deep water, but they also help them acti-vate their superpower: schooling.

From the outside, it seems like fish swim-ming in a school have somehow tapped into one another's brains and are able to move around as one giant fishy-brained creature. But from the inside, it's a mass of individual fishy brains, each making life-and-death decisions.

Fish swim in schools because being in a large group helps them avoid hungry predators, find food more easily, and connect with one another. In dark black-waters, tetras pick out other striped fishies to form their schools. Then, within the schools, each tetra tries to find the best swimming spot.

It works like this:

When tetras are hungry, they try to swim on the outside of the school so they can have the best chances at gobbling up food.

But when they're just swimming along, they try to hang back. That way they can catch the draft of the fish ahead of them and don't have to work so hard to swim. The fish in the front wave the water with their bodies, which makes a little current for the fish in the back to hop onto, sort of like one of those moving walkways at the airport.

When a predator rears its ugly head, each fish tries to squeedle into the middle of the pack. With any luck, they think, Chompers will nab an outside fish and leave them safe.

Watching a neon tetra school in your tank or in the wild can teach you a lot about what's happening with the fish. For example, neon tetras are masters at social distancing—especially when one gets sick. While they're happy to greet healthy-looking tetras, they avoid the sickies if they can. More space

between them could mean there's an illness in their midst.

Also, when neon tetras go to sleep, they cut off the lights on their stripes, and the shiny blue and red fade to gray and black, helping them hide in the dark waters while they catch some z's. Like your mama says, you need a good night's rest if you want to do well in school.

# Part V

# The Cage

With the exception of ferrets, most creatures that scurry about in cages are near the bottom of the food chain. They have to be sneaky if they want to live their best lives while not getting eaten, and they do it so well. They have songs that seem silent and languages made of stink, and sometimes they seem a little nutty if they're homesick. Time to eavesdrop!

# The Most Lovably Fierce Stink Wars

Though undeniably adorable, hamsters are not the visionaries of the rodent world. Mostly because their vision is pretty terrible. Near-sighted and color-blind, hamsters are easily startled by anyone coming to give them a fluffle-nuffle (which is what we call petting a hamster because to us they are little fluffle-nuffles who need us to fluffle-nuffle them).

Forget sight, though. Hamsters don't need to see in order to recognize each other. More than that, they don't need to see each other to have conversations. They can talk with smell. Tucked within each hamster's chubby flanks are scent glands. Lady Hamstalot uses her scent glands to say, "Come and get me, fellas!" When she's ready to  mate, she rubs her yummy tummy wherever she can, spreading her smell so the guys know where to find her.

But the males use the funks in their trunks a little differently. They scent mark to show that they are the biggest, baddest hamsters around. "Gwar! Take that! Don't mess with Sir Stink!" they grumble as they angrily plop their chubby tummies and rub their cute little legs all over the place. "Get a whiff of that! I'm one baaaaaaaad smeller!"

Meanwhile, Lady Hamstalot sniffs around for the smelliest male she can find. The more stink a hamster spreads, the more interested she gets—and the more likely she is to choose him as her hunky funky lover. That's why many males scurry around, rubbing their flanks over spots where other males have marked, trying to erase the other male's stink. That's also why male hamsters fight for dominance, biting each other's flanks in an effort to disrupt their rivals' stinkiness. Sometimes

they'll even gnaw off another male's stink glands to keep him from smelling up the place!

Although stink battles rage and can turn aggressive, hamster funk is designed to keep the peace. Often, if a male is stinky enough to win the smell contest, other males will recognize and respect He Who Is Smelliest and back off without a fight.

Saved by the smell.

# Home Sweet Home— Can You Dig It?

Most gerbil owners have noticed that Peanut spends a lot of time in the corner. Digging. Into the plastic. Plastic that does not allow for digging. Peanut never makes progress, but she still scrapes and scratches until she gets exhausted, stops for a little drink from the water bottle, and goes back to her hard work of digging a hole to nowhere. "Let it go, Peanut!" owners say. "Enjoy this bounty of nibbles and fluff you have been provided!"

But Peanut can't let it go. If we want to understand her mission to go underground, we need to  dig deep. A gerbil's desire to dig traces back to before her birth, to her ancestral deserts and shrublands in Mongolia, China, and Russia, where wild gerbils still frolic and peek from their tunnel homes.

In their wild desert hometowns, gerbils live underground, where it's cooler. At the end of their tunnels, they make chambers where they can keep food, hang out, and have babies. In the dry desert, gerbils sniff around for seeds and insects, and their quick little bodies make nice meals for predators like snakes and owls. Watch out, Wild Peanut!

To play it safe under-
ground, gerbils like a lot of
exits. To that end, they've
been known to excavate up
to twenty front and back
doors to their houses. Way to
keep 'em guessing, Wild Peanut.

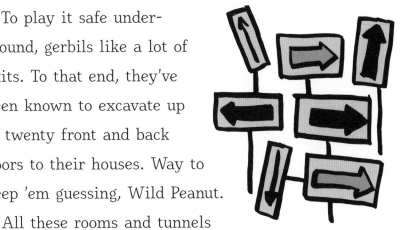

All these rooms and tunnels
take a lot of digging, but gerbils are no dummies.
If their mamas and papas have already made
them a nice home, complete with a decent
chamber connected to a good-enough tunnel, the
gerbils will leave good enough alone and stay in
their parents' houses when they grow up. But
Pet Peanut didn't grow up in tunnels. She probably grew up in a pet store or some person's
house, and that's where we can unearth clues to
the nonstop tunneling. See what we did there?
Unearth? Digging? Ahem. Moving on.

If a gerbil is born and raised in a happy,
regular, tunnel-free cage, she'll dig like her life

depends on it, even if you give her the tunnel and chamber of her dreams when she comes to live with you. BUT if she is born and raised in a happy little chamber connected to a tunnel, when she grows up, *she won't dig* in the corner, even if she doesn't have a tunnel to call her own.

Scientists think that's because when baby gerbils grow up without tunnels and chambers, the part of their little brains that they share with their relatives back in the dry lands of Mongolia develops a message that could save their lives if they were back in the wild.

"Peanut," your gerbil's brain tells her, "life is strange here. There are no tunnels for you. But you, Peanut, *you* are a rodent *built for tunnels*! What will you do with no tunnels?" Her brain continues (it's a long message), "Owls could eat you! You have no food storage room! No place to have babies! May this be your mission in life, Peanut! Bring back the tunnels to gerbildom, where you will reign *forever*!" Or something like that.

And so poor Peanut is left to excavate for the rest of her days. Or try to. You gotta hand it to her—she doesn't give up.

# Rise of the Adorable Poop Eaters

Bunnies and guinea pigs: Can it get any cuter?! Covered in soft fur, from their nubby little tails to the tips of their sniffy little noses. And just look at the way they nibble-nibble on their special vitamin-packed dookie balls. Yep. Our favorite furry sweetie pies secretly snack on BMs before giving us their morsel-like kisses from heaven. Calm down! Sure, go wash your face, but don't freak out. For one, they only eat *special* poop, and for another, they have to do it to stay alive.

Here's the deal. Guinea pigs and rabbits eat grasses. That's lucky for them because they are short, and in the wild, grass is abundant and at mouth level. It must be like swimming all day in an ice cream ocean. Or just imagine if your bed, your carpet, and everything around you were made of candy bars.
Oooh, or if your whole school were made of chicken nuggets (or tofu nuggets, if that's your thing). Or the walls were made of pizza slices. Need to stop dreaming . . . too much drooling . . .

Anyway, grass is pretty much everywhere, and guinea pigs and rabbits make good use of it. The trouble is that some of that grass is hard to digest. Humans can't digest it at all because we don't have the special bacteria in our bellies that can break down grass's most abundant compound: cellulose. Cows have the bacteria, but it still takes them *four stomachs* and lots of throwing up to digest grass. Rabbits and guinea

pigs have only one stomach, and they carry their cellulose-busting bacteria in their intestines.

When a rabbit or guinea pig eats, the food goes down its esophagus and through its belly, which breaks the food down as much as it can. What's left over travels into the hindgut, where the food meets its mineral makers. Enzymes ferment the undigested food-turned-poop, and the result

is a nice, vitamin-packed glob of dook called a cecotrope (SEE-coh-trohp), or night feces.

The trouble is, now that the cellulose is ready for the vitamins and minerals to be sucked out of it through digestion, it's all the way in the critter's hind end. It needs to be back in the critter's stomach, where digestion begins. There's an easy remedy for that: poop it out and gobble it again. Cecotropes look different from regular poop: they're darker and softer, more like poop pudding than poop cereal. Also, it's so important for the animal to gobble these nutrients that humans rarely see it happen. That's because rabbits and guinea pigs scarf their cecotrope down as quickly as they push it out. Without  their bacterial buddies and special yummy poop, guinea pigs and rabbits would become malnourished and die.

So where do baby rabbits and guinea pigs, new to the world and in need of microbes, get the bacteria to get their butt parties started? They eat their mothers' poop, of course. Lots of cute leaf lovers eat poop, too—not just rabbits and guinea pigs. Beavers, some opossums, and some lemurs all wait excitedly for delicious poop packets to emerge from their bottoms so they can have their favorite desserts.

# A Brief History of a Little Thief

The name *ferret* comes from the Latin word for "little thief." And yes, they've been known to pilfer and hide our stuff, but we humans did not begin to keep ferrets as pets so they would steal our socks. We started keeping ferrets thousands of years ago because they make good hunters.

Ferrets can be picky little carnivores. By the time they're six months old, they've imprinted on their favorite foods. This means that whatever they were eating as young ferrets is what they will prefer to eat forever. After six months, they often turn their noses up at anything that seems like an out-of-the-ordinary meal. To

today's ferret owner, this could mean that your weasel won't eat things you consider prime ferret cuisine. But, as you'll soon discover, to ferret owners of yore, this imprinting made for a super-valuable pet.

Because ferrets can squeeze their long, lean bodies into tunnels, and because they often like to eat things that drive us nuts—rats and garden-munching rabbits, for example—Julius Caesar ordered ancient Romans to use them as hunters to control rabbit plagues in 6 BCE. Ferrets worked so well as rabbit hunters that Romans brought them along to the new places they dominated.

Fellow global dominator Genghis Khan, ruler of the Mongols during the early 1200s, also enjoyed the sport of rabbit hunting with ferrets. If only the Romans and Mongols could have put down their spears and swords and enjoyed their strange shared pastime. How different the world would be! Just imagine! No rabbits, abundant weasels with their musky stench. The majority of us may never have been born because our forebears may never have met . . . Maybe it's better they didn't hug it out.

Ferret hunting continued to delight the English countryside in the 1300s. The English government made laws to restrict the ownership of ferrets for hunting to only the wealthiest landowners. A gentleman's pet. We aren't sure how the English enforced this fancy ferret-hunting rule, but we are sure that it is a weird rule and that it sounds like their government didn't have enough going on at the time.

As colonists began to spread to the western part of the United States in the 1800s, they brought their trusted ferrets with them to patrol their grain stores for rats and mice. Remember how ferrets pick  their favorite foods for life at an early age? Those home-home-on-the-range ferrets imprinted on rats and mice and spent their days ravenous for the pests they feasted on as youths. This made ferrets priceless pets on any homestead lucky enough to have them. You might not see them in movies about the Wild West, but right alongside those sheriffs, outlaws, horses, and saloons, furry little thieves were hard at work, sniffing out vermin and taking no prisoners.

# I Am Mouse, Hear Me Roar

If you spend a lot of time with mice, or if you imagine spending time with mice, you might hear them snuffle. You may even hear them squeak every now and again when they want you to leave them alone, for example, or when you startle them by sneaking up on them. Are you even someone who sneaks up on mice? Take it from us. They're easily startled. One minute they're off in their own worlds, digging their little mousy nests, daydreaming of giant peanut-butter-cheese-cracker sandwiches, and the next:

SQUEAK! Translation: "WHAWAZDAT?! YOU SCARED THE DAYLIGHTS OUT OF ME!" Don't sneak up on mice. They don't like it. It's mean.

Anyway, mice squeak when they want you to hear them, but mice have another language, a secret language, and they use it all day long. The thing is, you can't hear it.

We humans can hear plenty of things. We can hear our parents telling us to get out of bed already, we're going to be late for school. We can hear crickets chirping in our backyards, and birds hollering at each other from the power lines. But there are plenty of things we can't hear. That's because our range of hearing is limited to between 20 Hz and 20 kHz. "Twenty kwhutz?" you ask. Twenty kilohertz. A hertz is a measurement for audio frequency.

Close your eyes. Wait. Don't close your eyes. You can't read this if your eyes are closed. Just imagine a wave. Sound moves like a wave. Hertz is the measurement of the number of waves hitting your ears per second. So 1 hertz would be one long wave in one second. We can't hear that. It would be too low for us to detect. That's called the infrasonic range. Elephants send low messages in the infrasonic range, far across the savannas. Giraffes, too.

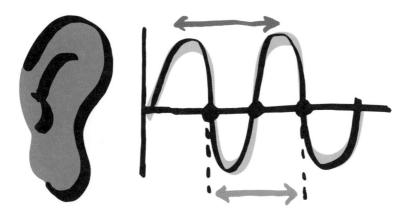

Twenty kilohertz means that 20,000 of those little waves hit our ears each second. Frequencies above that are beyond our ability to hear. Mice can chitchat at up to 40 kilohertz. You can strain those ears all you want, but you're never gonna hear it, no matter how loud it is.

They're saying all kinds of things to each other that we can't hear. Mice are sociable animals, as far as rodents go. They some-times hang out, scarfle down food together, have parties in your walls while you sleep. You know, sociable. Conversations make it much easier to socialize, and mice are excellent conversationalists.

A mama mouse will gather her babies when they peep out a "Mama, where are you?" call. Mice get frightened when they hear the secret distress calls from their mousy neighbors. Girl mice squeak "go away!" calls to boy mice that keep showing up uninvited. But they all save their best squeaks for their mating calls. Male mice have roars that could rival the roars coming from the manliest manes of the African savannas.

Male mice, when they're in the mood for love, sing songs they hope will attract the most gorgeous lady mouse around. And by around, we mean pretty much *anywhere* around. Males are *loud*. Their rodent roars can  be up to 100 decibels loud. That's as loud as a jackhammer, or a helicopter 100 feet (30 meters) over your head, or a motorcycle. It's something you just couldn't miss—if you could only hear it.

In some mouse species, the females who like that music will sing back, just as loud, to deter other lady mice who might start getting ideas about wanting that hot crooner down the alley. They sing their love songs in this way, louder than garbage trucks rumbling by, as loud as a tractor. They sing, hopeful for love, all around us while we turn over on our pillows and enjoy a nice, sound sleep.

# Part VI

# The Terrarium

We know not everyone loves reptiles, amphibians, or arthropods. But that's only because they don't know better—yet. Each of our slithery, scaled, or crawly pets has its own top-secret hacks, charms, and fears, whether it's having nightmares of a body snatcher or knowing how to blend in if you can't change clothes. It's time to get the deets.

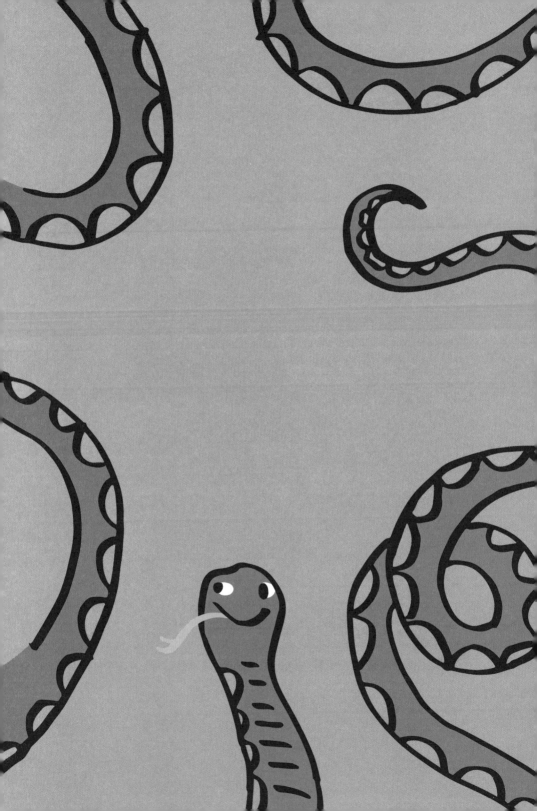

# Butterfingers
# Superspy

Corn snakes are pretty slick. All snakes are slick, we suppose, with no hands or feet and all that sliding they do. But we mean corn snakes are like James Bond slick. Agent 007 (that's James Bond's secret agent number) has to save the day while at the same time escaping from the clutches of the villains out to get him. To do this, he often needs to avoid detection. That's not easy. James Bond's a good-lookin' dude who somehow manages to blend in with his surroundings on his superspy missions, even though he wears a tuxedo pretty much everywhere he goes.

How does a fetching fella blend in if he's wearing a tuxedo? He goes to a fancy-dress party with plenty of fetching fellas wearing tuxedos.

Like James Bond, corn snakes often need to blend in. For one, they don't have sharp teeth or venom, which makes them tasty snacks for predators. For another, they hunt for food such as small birds and mammals, and they have to be sneaky-sneaky to avoid detection. But, like 007 and his tuxedo, corn snakes have only one outfit.

Corn snakes come in an array of colors and patterns in the wild and, thanks to crafty corn snake breeders, even more colors in captivity. In their southeastern United States habitat, they live in fields, forests, and old buildings.

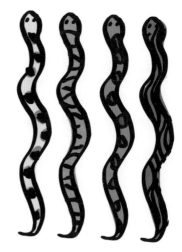

These fields, forests, and old buildings have
plenty of colors and patterns within them, just
like the snakes. Think of how sunlight dapples
a forest floor, leaving some areas shadowy and
some bright. And how the rusty pine straw
makes the ground in one place a different color
than the tree bark, sandy paths, gravel, and
maple leaves scattered in another.

Corn snakes can see these differences, too.
They also know which color tuxedo they're
wearing. So when it's time to hide, they slide
into a backdrop that matches their bodies.
Reddish snakes slither in
the pine straw; dusty-
looking ones remain
still on the path.
By hiding in the
surroundings that
blend with their
scales, they become
almost invisible to passersby.

That's where their supersmooth spy behavior comes to a halt, though. Remember, corn snakes don't have venom. They kill their prey by constricting it.

In case you wanted to constrict your own supper, here's a handy guide:

1.  Throw a surprise party. By that we mean be as quiet as possible. When you see your supper, like a juicy mouse, leap out. And instead of yelling "SURPRISE," chomp down on its head so it can't breathe that well.

2.  Give it a hug. We mean wrap yourself around that mouse's body as tight as you can and squeeeeeeeze. Every time it breathes out, squeeeeze a little tighter so its breaths become shallower and shallower.

3. Wait. It'll stop breathing soon enough. Then, if you're a corn snake reading this, you can unhook your jaw and start to swallow that mouse whole.

If you're a person reading this, don't do any of these things. Just eat regular food the regular way. You have plenty of other opportunities in life to be creative.

It's not easy to tie yourself in knots like corn snakes need to do to squeeze the life out of their suppers in step two. And corn snakes aren't born knowing how to do it. They learn through practice, and they drop a lot of prey along the way.

Young corn snakes start life by nabbing reptiles and amphibians as small as they are. As the snakes grow, they work their way up to birds and mammals. Sometimes they sneak up

to mama birds sleeping in their
nests, gently nudge them off
their babies, and slip off
with baby-bird suppers.
Devious!

As their prey grows
more complicated, so do the
hairpin loops, twists, and knots they
need to tie themselves into
to give the big squeeze.
It's like a ballet of
death, and the best-fed
snakes are the
nimblest, whether in
the terrarium or in the
wild.

By the time they're swallowing mice (squeezed,
not shaken *or* stirred), they're matching their
bodies to their backgrounds like 007 at a cocktail
party. Mission accomplished.

# Have a Ball, Baby

One of the reasons we keep ball pythons as pets is that they are sweetie peeties. Or, at least, unlike many other snakes, when it comes to whether they will bite your face off or run and hide, they usually choose to hide. More specifically, they choose to curl up in as tight a ball as they can and tuck their heads in the middle in a "You can't see me if I can't see you" fashion. Or maybe it's a "No snake here! Just this pile of leaf-looking scaly stuff that is definitely not a snake!" fashion. Either way, it's the most lovable of all possible snake responses, and we humans find it both irresistible and convenient from a "Won't get my face bitten off if I keep this snake" perspective.

Ball pythons don't use up all their ball power on fear, though. Mother ball pythons also use it for making the best babies they can. Here's what happens: After Mother Ball lays her eggs (usually between one and eleven at a time), she makes a nice little egg pile and wraps herself around it in a ball.

Snakes are, in general, ectotherms, or cold-blooded. That means instead of generating heat inside their bodies, they use the sun and the warmth of the world around them as their furnace. Some snake species, like larger pythons, can make their own heat when they incubate their eggs, but not ball pythons. Even when they're warming babies, they're still using the world around them to keep the heat running.

That means Mother Ball has two jobs: First, she uses her camouflaged skin and super-ball superpowers to hide her eggs' bright white shells from egg-eating predators. Second, she needs to keep her eggs from drying out. By curling up into a ball, she becomes a living ziplock baggie, sealing in their freshness with her patented mama-wrap. The mamas who are better at wrapping have fatter, squirmier babies—another genera-tion of sweetie peeties.

# You Can Change the Textbooks

## An Interview with Warren Booth

Warren Booth is a snake guy. And a lizard guy. And a bug guy. And a turtle guy. And a dog person. And a rock musician. And a—look, he's into a lot of things. An associate professor of evolutionary genetics at the University of

Oklahoma in Tulsa, he's enthusiastic about life, and he's found that when he pursues the things he loves, he makes big discoveries.

Following a hunch he had about pet boa constrictors, Warren used science to uncover information that would forever change the way we think about how snakes make babies. We'll let him tell you more about how it all happened, but first, we want to tell you what he learned.

Warren discovered that some female snakes can reproduce by parthenogenesis (PAR-thuh-noh-JEH-nuh-sus). That means the mothers can make babies even if they have not mated with a male. The babies have no father.

Many creatures need fathers to give copies of their genes to mothers so that the two sets of genes can combine to form a baby, but for some snakes (and sharks, and birds, and other reptiles), daddies aren't necessarily required.

Warren was the first to discover that boa constrictors are daddy-optional. After that, he and his team found that other snakes—including pythons, rattlesnakes, copperheads, cottonmouths, garter snakes, and even king cobras—don't always need a male to reproduce.

While a female snake would likely prefer to have a partner to make babies, in some cases it might not work out. For example, what if she's a pet or a zoo snake and doesn't have access to males? Or imagine she's washed out to sea and lands on an island with no other snakes like her. She needs more snakes! Why not just make more?

**"Parthenogenesis in reptiles might even go further back in time in the evolutionary tree of life," says Warren. "It would not be hard to believe that dinosaurs could produce parthenogenetically. Life finds a way . . ."**

Like most great researchers, Warren always finds a way to follow his curiosity. We'll let him tell you about it.

You have studied all kinds of animals, from bedbugs to mole crickets and more. How did you make the leap to snakes?

"I grew up in a house where we always had pets. In fact, my parents even owned a pet store for a short time when I was young.

"This love of animals and nature stuck with me as I grew older and became fascinated by genetics—specifically how different traits, like an animal's colors and patterns, are inherited. So I started studying evolutionary genetics in school.

"I loved betta fish. At home, I would breed different colors and patterns to see what their offspring would look like. Then, when I was about sixteen years old, I saw a

pet snake in an enclosure and was fascinated. I went straight home and asked my mum if I could get a reptile. She said sure, and we got a leopard gecko . . . then another . . . then a snake . . . then another, then another. And now, well, I have many, many snakes.

"How this led to my current work on snakes is quite fortuitous. I was in a lab working on urban pest insects when a friend called me and asked if it was possible to do a paternity test on a boa constrictor. My friend wanted to find out which male that they had paired their female with was the father of the resulting babies.

"It just so happened that I had recently developed genetic markers for boas that would allow me to do this. So my friend collected some shed skins from the mother, the babies, and the possible fathers, and I extracted DNA from the skins and tested them. To my amazement, my genetic tests revealed that the babies were all partial clones of the mother. That means they had no father!

"When zoos and other snake-keepers learned about what we did from the news, they began to contact me, telling me about unusual events they'd witnessed where snakes had been held in isolation for long periods of time and suddenly gave birth.

"We were able to conduct many studies on this, and, as a result, we have also been able to advance our understanding of other aspects of snake biology. My discoveries have led people to totally rewrite biology textbooks!

"So, a simple phone call from a friend asking if I could do a paternity test on a snake led us to totally revolutionize that aspect of snake biology."

What is your favorite part of your research?

"My favorite part about science, in general, is finding out things that nobody knew before. Until only a few years ago, many people had no idea that parthenogenesis like this could happen in snakes and in many other creatures. And yet it happens in birds and sharks and reptiles. In fact, it might even have happened in dinosaurs! How cool is that?! The fact that this work is rewriting textbooks is very exciting.

"My proudest moment, however, was sitting with my daughter, watching a David Attenborough documentary. In that show, he talked about parthenogenesis, then talked about my work on pit vipers. That was really cool."

# Worst-Case Scenario: Call the Sentinels of Doom

This is the story of some once-loved pets and the turmoil and destruction they can cause when humans decide they no longer wish to care for their snakes.

If you're sort of into snakes, you might think a young Burmese python would make a good pet. After all, they're easy enough to buy. Many pet stores and breeders across the United States sell them at an affordable price. You might also think, "They're not venomous. That means they won't kill me if they bite me." Instead of venom, they have backward-facing, extremely pointy teeth they use to grab their victims by the head. Once they have their victims in their grasp, Burmese pythons wrap their bodies around them, smother their faces, and squeeze the life out of them.

When these snakes are little, it's not so bad. You can throw a dead rat into the cage, pat Sir Hiss on the back, and call it a month. The

 trouble is, Burmese pythons don't stay little—and few of us have enough room to contain or enough large animals to feed a 20-foot (6-meter) snake. When they get too big to keep at the house, many people

find themselves at a loss for what to do with their pets. It's hard to find a home for a snake that size. It's a puzzle! Many folks have solved this problem by sending their slithery pets on a permanent vacation to the Florida Everglades.

Ah, the Florida Everglades. More than 2 million acres of wilderness at Florida's tip, 100 miles (160 kilometers) long and 50 miles (80 kilometers) wide.  Throughout the mangrove forests and limestone islands, panthers prowl, manatees graze, more than 360 species of birds flit and chirp, deer frolic, and alligators lurk. Because the Everglades work as a giant water filtration and purification system—in addition to being home to all those creatures and plants—we would be lost without these wetlands. They provide clean drinking water for an entire third of Floridians and irrigation for much of the state's farmland.

Another creature lives there now, too—an ex-pet that threatens to rip apart the fabric of nature. Our Burmese pythons slither through the mangroves and tall grasses, devouring nearly everything in their paths. They are native to Southeast Asia. The creatures of the Everglades have no natural fear of them.

They should. Burmese pythons have swallowed up to 99 percent of the Everglades' small

mammals. These snakes were first released in the Everglades by pet owners who thought they were being kindhearted. About the time Sir Hiss starts hungrily eyeballing the family cat, people realize they should maybe have gotten something smaller. A corn snake, perhaps. Or a nice fat hamster. But what to do with Sir Hiss? They can't let him *starve*. And nobody else wants him!

It turns out that plenty of people have a plan for this. They let their Sir Hisses free. Run, Sir Hiss! Run like the wind! Run wild! Or slither. People have dumped enough of their Sir Hisses and Lady Hisses near the Everglades that by the 1990s, these snakes had started finding one another and having baby Hisses. Now there are uncountable hungry Hisses in the Everglades.

So far, researchers have found raccoons, opossums, thirty-seven species of birds, bobcats, rabbits, and even whole deer in python bellies.

What can we do? Scientists have tried shooting them with guns, but the snakes are sneaky and hard to find. Their colors blend in well with the Everglades' hues, and they're good swimmers. If you spook Lady Hiss in the water, she can dive down and hold her breath for up to 30 minutes while she waits for you to forget about her.

To outsneak these sneaky snakes, scientists have gotten *sneakier*. They invented what we are calling the Sentinels of Doom. (Scientists call them "sentinel snakes," but we don't feel like that tells the whole story.)

Pinpointing and eliminating one snake at a time can take days, so researchers figured out how to use these Sentinels of Doom to find a bunch of them at once. First, scientists implant a little tracking device in a captured male python. That's the Sentinel of Doom snake. A sentinel is a soldier that keeps watch for trouble, and the Sentinel of Doom snake does just that. He leads researchers to a big pile o' slithers.

When it's time for Burmese pythons to mate, the female puts out a chemical trail that lures males from all around. They slither to her and pile around her, hoping to be the father of the next batch of opossum eaters. In these mating balls, bunches of males gather, fertilizing up to 100 eggs in that one mama snake.

The Sentinel of Doom is an otherwise ordinary snake, hoping to be a baby daddy with the rest of the pack. Except when he follows the female's trail, his tracking device tells the researchers where he is, so they can follow the trail, too. Sentinels of Doom have led researchers to many snake parties, including one with six males surrounding a 115-pound (52-kilogram) female. All non-sentinels were

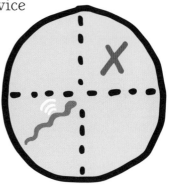

eliminated, but the sentinels were released so they could continue doing their dastardly good deeds for the Everglades.

No one knows exactly how many

Burmese pythons are skulking around the Everglades. In many places, the land is too wild for humans to enter. We do know that Sentinels of Doom are doing their jobs, but many, many snakes remain. A lot of work lies ahead. In the meantime, we know what *not* to do when it comes to getting rid of unwanted pets. Remember Sir Hiss.

# Your Tarantula's Worst Nightmare

We know this might be hard to believe, but some people are afraid of spiders. Like, really afraid of them. They're afraid to leave their mouths open when they sleep because they think a spider's going to crawl in there. ("And then what?" we ask. "Brush your teeth?") They're afraid to walk in the basement because they think a spider's going to drop down on them. ("And then what?" we ask. "Say 'BOO!'?") They're afraid that any spider crawling across their living room rug is actually mounting an assault against them. ("AND THEN WHAT?!?!" we ask. "IS IT GOING TO EAT YOU???")*

If you own a spider, you know how their chirpy approach to life and sometimes sassy attitudes can bring joy to any household. Still, it makes sense that some people think spiders are a little creepy. Spiders are predators, after all. They have all those legs. They're always sneaking around, lurking in caverns and corners.

---

*Full disclosure: We used to be very afraid of spiders. All these fears and more were our own fears. If you are afraid of spiders like we *used to be*, it might be helpful to try what worked for us. First, we learned about the spiders living around us. We learned what they were doing, how they behaved, what they ate, and more. Then we watched them. It turns out that spiders are pretty cool! They're helpful, they're always up to something, and they can be nice house-mates. Make friends with your spiders!

Plus, they do have fangs. But here's the thing: spiders do not want to eat us. They would rather we just left them alone to enjoy their creepy little caves, corners, and crevices in peace. Besides, spiders have much more to worry about than how to spook and devour their human housemates. Tarantulas know this better than anybody. They might seem like the stuff of nightmares, with their ginormous fangs and even ginormous-er bodies. Tarantulas have fears, too. Unlike our worries, spider worries are a matter of life and death.

While we go to sleep trying to keep our mouths closed so the spider on the windowsill doesn't come brush our teeth, the tarantula in our terrarium might want to sleep with one eye open if it knows what's good for it. Tarantulas have eight eyes, after all, so leaving one open shouldn't be that big of a deal. Actually, they don't have eyelids, so their eyes are open all the time. The point is, they should be afraid. Very afraid.

To understand your tarantula's worst nightmare, you first need to know about your spider's natural habitat and its spidey skills. When they're not living with us, tarantulas prowl around in warm-weather regions all over the world. Some are as small as those green peas you stuff under your mashed potatoes, and others are as big as the dinner plate your peas and potatoes sit on. They all like to hunt. They eat creatures ranging in size from small insects to birds and bats.

Look at your spider's body. It's equipped with plenty of things to help with happy hunting. It has excellent vision, as far as spiders go. It has lightning-quick reflexes, mostly because it detects air movement with special hairs all over its body. It can *feel* you coming before it *sees* you coming.

It has retractable, catlike claws that help it handle prey and climb. It has huge fangs that pump venom into its meals. The venom from most tarantulas could hurt a human, but it won't hurt for long (unless the human is allergic). Their venom can't kill anybody bigger than a bat. Are you bigger than a bat? Yes? Whew!

Some tarantula bodies also come equipped with extra tools that help hungry spider eaters remember who's boss. Tarantulas living in the Americas can kick irritating little hairs off their bodies, flicking them at would-be offenders. "Take that!" they say, kicking their hairs as they run away.

Still, none of these spidey powers, not their hair flinging nor their creepiness nor their fangs, is any defense against tarantulas' worst nightmare: the tarantula hawk.

The tarantula hawk isn't really a hawk. It's a wasp. It's not just one wasp, but lots of different species of wasps, as varied in style and habitat as tarantulas are. But all tarantula hawks love one thing: tarantulas.

Tarantula hawks are in the scientific tribe Pepsini. They are shaped like the wasps you see building nests under the eaves in your doorway, except much larger and usually a beautiful iridescent green-blue color. They also have massively long stingers, their instruments for tarantula destruction.

Just imagine that your pet tarantula, Claude, was born in the wild and not in captivity. Instead of living in your bedroom, he scurries across the wildlands. "I love it here!" Claude says to himself as he makes his little silken tarantula tunnel hut underground. "Life is amazing!" Clearly, because Claude lives in the wild and not with you, he doesn't know how fantastic it is to live with you. If he did, he wouldn't be saying such things. Claude also doesn't know that Madame Pepsini has already found him. She is sneakier than Claude is quick. Before Claude can rear up to reveal his fangs or scoot farther down his tunnel hut, Madame P stings him between the legs.

"That really hurt!" says Claude, who doesn't quite realize his life is about to get 1,000 percent awful. "Why would you . . . do . . . sommmmethinghhblaaaaaaaaaaaaahhhh."

He starts talking like that at the end because Madame P has paralyzed him with her venom. Not killed him, mind you. That would interfere with her dastardly plan. He is still painfully alive but unable to protest as the rest of his short and horrific life unfolds before him.

First, Madame P drags the limp and helpless
Claude to a tunnel she dug just for him. She
tucks him in nice and tight and lays one tiny egg
on his body. Then she leaves him forever, sealing
him in his underground grave.

The nightmare has only just begun.

What happens next? Madame P's baby, Li'l P,
hatches from the egg. Tiny, grublike, and very
hungry, Li'l P makes the smallest of holes in
Claude's body, careful not to kill him. She wiggles
inside. Then she starts to eat. And eat. And eat.
She gobbles Claude's insides day and night and
does not touch any of his vital organs as she eats.
She wants to keep him alive, you see. She doesn't
want a rotting carcass to eat. She likes her meat
fresh.

Poor Claude cannot protest as Li'l P chomps
through his body, doubling, tripling, quadrupling
in size. When she gets large enough and ready
to pupate, she finally gives Claude the mercy
she's been denying him. She eats his vital organs,

killing him and turning his body into a safe chamber for her to transform into an adult.

Eventually, she bursts out of the husk that was once Claude, having transformed his happy insides into her own sleek form. Li'l P will go on to hunt more tarantulas. Claude had no time to warn the others about his fate, but some strange feeling still must linger in those tarantulas that remain, even those living in our homes. Are they pacing their tanks because they are hungry? Or because they have an eerie feeling they're being stalked? Maybe you have felt that same unease when you turn on the basement light or peer into the dark beneath your bed. A nightmare that you just can't seem to shake.

Thankfully, your pet Claude lives with you, safe from the stings of Madame P. Maybe. Keep the lid on that terrarium tight, just in case.

# Color Fight!

Bearded dragons are one of the most popular lizard pets. It's not hard to see why. With their spiky manes and friendly, curious expressions, they look like mad scientists who just got struck by lightning but are somehow pleased with the situation. Bearded dragons also have the power to change color, and they can do it for brilliant reasons.

Godzilla (that's our bearded dragon's name. We mean, if we had a bearded dragon, that would be his name. Let us dream!) is able to change colors because he has these cells in his body called chromatophores (kroh-MA-tuh-fors), which hold pigment. Pigment is like ink for skin.

Godzilla's chromatophores can scatter that pigment or bring it together whenever he wants, and that's how he's able to change colors. It's like if you had a white balloon with black liquid ink inside that was under your command. "All ink rise to the surface!" you might say, and the ink would come to the top of the balloon and the balloon would look almost black. "All ink spread throughout my balloon!" you might say, and the liquid would float around the balloon's center, and from the outside the balloon would look gray, or even

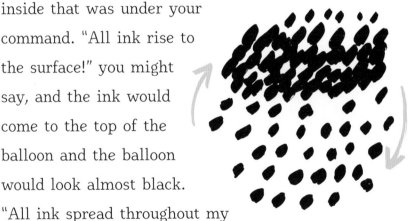

white. Except Godzilla has inky balloon-type cells throughout his skin. He can go from dark gray to bright yellow. Some bearded dragons can even be a rusty color.

When it's time for males to scuffle over a lady, bearded dragons try changing colors before coming to blows. Make way for Hydra, the loveliest lady lizard in town. All the male bearded dragons want to make Hydra their lizard bride, but first, they must battle for her affections. Godzilla and Uncle Deadly each believe that they would be the best mate for the enchanting Hydra.

The two males approach each other, spreading out their scaly collars and getting those chromatophores to be as close to black as they can.

"You don't wanna mess with this," Godzilla says as he reveals his darkest dark side.

"Oh yeah?" says his rival, Uncle Deadly. "You don't wanna mess with THIS!" And he shows just how dark he can go.

They stare at each other. They think about it. Uncle Deadly is clearly darker. Godzilla  considers this. He looks at Hydra as she tries unsuccessfully to eat a grasshopper. Perhaps she is not as dreamy as he first imagined. Also, Uncle Deadly is one scary dragon.

"You win!" Godzilla yelps as he scuttles away.

By having darkest-beard battles, bearded dragons can see how powerful other dragons might be without resorting to a knock-down, drag-out fight. That's because these beard battles show, without fighting, that the dragon is either (a) big enough to have a larger swath of dark-ness on his massive beard than his opponent or (b) well fed and fit enough to make his darkness darker than his opponent's. The opponent—in this case, Godzilla—can see what he'd be getting into without actually having to get into it. It keeps them both safe and in one piece.

Avoiding blows isn't the bearded dragon's only colorful superpower. They also use their color powers to regulate their body temperature. Pretty cool, right? When it's hot outside, bearded dragons change their whole bodies to become lighter in color, and when it's colder, they'll grow darker. It's like wearing a black T-shirt in the sunshine. Their darker colors absorb more heat than lighter colors, helping them get toasty. On the other hand, wearing a white T-shirt in hot sun reflects heat, which helps your body temperature stay lower. Godzilla doesn't need a T-shirt, though. He's got it colored—we mean, covered.

# But Wait! There's More!

Your pets have so much more to tell you! And you have so much more you need to know! Here are some great places to go and things to read to help you expose the truth in your pets' hidden lives.

## Want to read more about pets?

First, if you are considering working with animals as a job, you have approximately 50 gazillion opportunities awaiting you. It's useful to master the lingo of your field so you'll know where to begin the hunt for your dream job.

A person who studies reptiles and amphibians is a **herpetologist.** One of the best ways to learn about snakes, frogs, and their relatives is to open a guidebook. In addition to getting nice viewing material, you'll get to see what different herps (that's what herpetologists call the animals they study) look like, what they eat, and where you might find them.

To learn more about snakes, check out Whit Gibbons and Mike Dorcas's *Snakes of the Southeast*, which is easy to read and has excellent

 photographs; Chris Mattison's *Snake: The Essential Visual Guide*, which provides plenty of anatomy info and a more global perspective; and Mark O'Shea's *The Book of Snakes: A Life-Size Guide to Six Hundred Species from Around the World*, which has a title that speaks for itself.

If you're more of a frog person, Tim Halliday's *The Book of Frogs: A Life-Size Guide to Six*

*Hundred Species from Around the World* is like that really cool snake book we mentioned, except it's about frogs and toads.

Want to go all in on herpetology guides? Check out the *Peterson Field Guide to Reptiles and Amphibians of Eastern and Central North America* and the *Peterson Field Guide to Western Reptiles and Amphibians.*

While it's fun to learn more about creatures that live nearby, don't limit yourself to guidebooks about animals in your region of the world. Sometimes the dreamiest guides direct you to places you'd like to visit. Do a search for guides to reptiles and amphibians in locales you imagine visiting one day, and take that nature hike of your dreams.

A person who studies insects and spiders is called an **entomologist**. More specifically, someone who studies spiders like your pet taran-tula is called an **arachnologist**. Plenty of spider books can get you going on how to iden-tify the spiders around you. Whether or not you live in Britain, the book *Britain's Spiders: A Field Guide* by Lawrence Bee, Geoff Oxford, and Helen Smith will give you an amazing look at how to find, collect, or just watch spiders. And my book with Christopher M. Buddle, *Dr. Eleanor's Book of Common Spiders*, shares tales of some of North America's most common spider species. Via the illustrated pages of Richard A. Bradley and Steve Buchanan's *Common Spiders of North America*, you could spend years just enjoying the beauty of arachnids.

Stanley A. Schultz and Marguerite J. Schultz's *The Tarantula Keeper's Guide: Comprehensive Information on Care, Housing, and Feeding* can help ensure you're taking the best care of your tarantula that you possibly can.

Spiders aren't the only pet arachnids, though, and Jillian Cowles talks about most of them in her book *Amazing Arachnids*.

A person who studies birds is called an **ornithologist**, and if you want to begin looking for birds, check out any of David Allen Sibley's guidebooks or his fascinating *What It's Like to Be a Bird*. If you're more interested in birds of the caged variety, David Alderton's *The Complete Practical Guide to Pet and Aviary Birds* can get you rolling.

A person who studies dogs can be called a **cynologist**, but most people just refer to themselves by the *way* they study dogs, like "animal behaviorist" or "pet psychologist" or "dog trainer" or "veterinarian." Consider Cat Warren's *What the*

*Dog Knows, Young Readers Edition: Scent, Science, and the Amazing Ways Dogs Perceive the World* and Aline Alexander Newman and Gary Weitzman's *How to Speak Dog: A Guide to Decoding Dog Language*. Sarah Albee's *Dog Days of History: The Incredible Story of Our Best Friends* shares the history of your best waggy buds.

A person who studies cats is called a **felinologist**, but, like people who study dogs, they usually just refer to themselves by the way they study cats. Aline Alexander Newman and Gary Weitzman's *How to Speak Cat* can get you started on your journey to chat up your cat.

A person who studies rodents like hamsters, mice, and gerbils is called a **rodentologist**, but they're like cat and dog people and usually refer to themselves by the way they study the animals. Patricia Bartlett's *The Hamster Handbook*, Ben Little's *Pet Mice: Your Pet Mouse Happy Care Guide*, Donna Anastasi's *Gerbils: The Complete Guide to Gerbil Care*, Bob Bennett's *Storey's Guide to Raising Rabbits*, and Immanuel Birmelin's *Guinea Pigs* should have you covered on your excellent pet care journey.

## Want to do some actual scientific research on animals from the comfort of your home (or yard or classroom)?

You'll be a great citizen scientist! A citizen scientist is a person who helps contribute data to real scientific studies. Scientists sometimes ask questions that they need a lot of help answering.

Help from YOU. At **zooniverse.org** and **scistarter.org**, your input makes a difference. Whether you're into microbes or animal behavior or Egyptology, these folks have your scientific curiosity covered. Try helping out with one of their studies! You'll like it! And if you don't like it, try another study!

## Want to draw a tapeworm with a flea as a pet who has a dog as a pet?

You're in luck. Rob Wilson knows just how to show you.

Once they're on the ground, tapeworms don't actually eat the poop. The part of the tapeworm in the poop pile is really a segment of the adult that's still in the dog's intestines, and the segment is filled with eggs. It's able to wiggle until it dries out and the eggs burst forth into the world, hoping a flea will eat them.

**First**

**Next**

**Then**

**Finally**

## Don't stop now!

If you want to check out some of the research the
scientists did to find out all this cool stuff, you
can visit their labs' websites or read the actual,
real-live studies! Here are a bunch of those
studies that we used to tell you stories about pets.

# Bibliography

## Part I: Dogs

### Talk to the Tail

Hecht, Julie, and Alexandra Horowitz. "Introduction to Dog Behavior." In *Animal Behavior for Shelter Veterinarians and Staff*, edited by Emily Weiss, Heather Mohan-Gibbons, and Stephen Zawistowski, 3–30. Hoboken, NJ: John Wiley & Sons, 2015. https://doi.org/10.1002/9781119421313.ch1.

Marshall-Pescini, Sarah, Franka S. Schaebs, Alina Gaugg, Anne Meinert, Tobias Deschner, and Friederike Range. "The Role of Oxytocin in the Dog–Owner Relationship." *Animals* 9, no. 10 (2019): 792. https://doi.org/10.3390/ani9100792.

Quaranta, A., M. Siniscalchi, and G. Vallortigara. "Asymmetric Tail Wagging Responses by Dogs to Different Emotive Stimuli." *Current Biology* 17, no. 6 (2007): R199–R201. https://doi.org/10.1016/j.cub.2007.02.008.

Sanni, Somppi, Heini Törnqvist, József Topál, et al. "Nasal Oxytocin Treatment Biases Dogs' Visual Attention and Emotional Response toward Positive Human Facial Expressions." *Frontiers in Psychology* 8, article no. 1854 (2017). https://doi.org/10.3389/fpsyg.2017.01854.

### True North, Poo North

Bartölke, Rabea, Heide Behrmann, Katharina Görtemaker, et al. "The Secrets of Cryptochromes: Photoreceptors, Clock Proteins, and Magnetic Sensors." *Neuroforum* 27, no. 3 (2021): 151–157. https://doi.org/10.1515/nf-2021-0006.

Beach, Frank A., and Robert W. Gilmore. "Response of Male Dogs to Urine from Females in Heat." *Journal of Mammalogy* 30, no. 4 (1949): 391–392. https://doi.org/10.2307/1375215.

Brown, Donna S., and Robert E. Johnston. "Individual Discrimination on the Basis of Urine in Dogs and Wolves." In *Chemical Signals in Vertebrates 3*, edited by Dietland Müller-Schwarze and Robert M. Silverstein, 343–346. Boston: Springer, 1983. https://doi.org/10.1007/978-1-4757-9652-0_28.

Gould, James L. "Animal Navigation." *Current Biology* 14, no. 6 (2004): R221–R224. https://doi.org/10.1016/j.cub.2004.02.049.

Hart, Vlastimil, Petra Nováková, Erich Pascal Malkemper, et al. "Dogs Are Sensitive to Small Variations of the Earth's Magnetic Field." *Frontiers in Zoology* 10, article no. 80 (2013). https://doi.org/10.1186/1742-9994-10-80.

Lohmann, Kenneth J. "Sea Turtles: Navigating with Magnetism." *Current Biology* 17, no. 3 (2007): R102–R104. https://doi.org/10.1016/j.cub.2007.01.023.

McGuire, B., B. Olsen, K. E. Bemis, and D. Orantes. "Urine Marking in Male Domestic Dogs: Honest or Dishonest?" *Journal of Zoology* 306, no. 3 (2018): 163–170. https://doi.org/10.1111/jzo.12603.

Meyer, Carl G., Kim N. Holland, and Yannis P. Papastamatiou. "Sharks Can Detect Changes in the Geomagnetic Field." *Journal of the Royal Society Interface* 2, no. 2 (2005): 129–130. https://doi.org/10.1098/rsif.2004.0021.

## Worst-Case Scenario: A Tale of Two Wormies / Doggie Howlser, MD

Dobler, Gerhard, and Martin Pfeffer. "Fleas as Parasites of the Family Canidae." *Parasites & Vectors* 4, article no. 139 (2011). https://doi.org/10.1186/1756-3305-4-139.

Hart, Benjamin L., and Lynette A. Hart. "How Mammals Stay Healthy in Nature: The Evolution of Behaviours to Avoid Parasites and Pathogens." *Philosophical Transactions of the Royal Society B* 373, no. 1751 (2018). https://doi.org/10.1098/rstb.2017.0205.

Hart, Benjamin L., Lynette A. Hart, Abigail P. Thigpen, Alisha Tran, and Melissa J. Bain. "The Paradox of Canine Conspecific Coprophagy." *Veterinary Medicine and Science* 4, no. 2 (2018): 106–114. https://doi.org/10.1002/vms3.92.

Hart, Benjamin L., and Karen L. Powell. "Antibacterial Properties of Saliva: Role in Maternal Periparturient Grooming and in Licking Wounds." *Physiology & Behavior* 48, no. 3 (1990): 383–386. https://doi.org/10.1016/0031-9384(90)90332-X.

Hoch, Heather, and Keith Strickland. "Canine and Feline Dirofilariasis: Life Cycle, Pathophysiology, and Diagnosis." *Compendium: Continuing Education for Veterinarians* 30, no. 3 (2008): 133–140. https://pubmed.ncbi.nlm.nih.gov/18409140/.

Huffman, M. A., and J. M. Caton. "Self-Induced Increase of Gut Motility and the Control of Parasitic Infections in Wild Chimpanzees." *International Journal of Primatology* 22 (2001): 329–346. https://doi.org/10.1023/A: 1010734310002.

Ledesma, Nicholas, and Laura Harrington. "Mosquito Vectors of Dog Heartworm in the United States: Vector Status and Factors Influencing Transmission Efficiency." *Topics in Companion Animal Medicine* 26, no. 4 (2011): 178–185. https://doi.org/10.1053/j.tcam.2011.09.005.

### SorryNotSorry—Don't Fall for That Guilty Look

Hecht, Julie, Ádám Miklósi, and Márta Gácsi. "Behavioral Assessment and Owner Perceptions of Behaviors Associated with Guilt in Dogs." *Applied Animal Behaviour Science* 139, nos. 1–2 (2012): 134–142. https://doi.org/10 .1016/j.applanim.2012.02.015.

# Part II: Cats

## Home on the Range

Cecchetti, Martina, Sarah L. Crowley, Cecily E. D. Goodwin, and Robbie A. McDonald. "Provision of High Meat Content Food and Object Play Reduce Predation of Wild Animals by Domestic Cats *Felis catus*." *Current Biology* 31, no. 5 (2021): 1107–1111. https://doi.org/10.1016/j.cub.2020.12.044.

Horn, Jeff A., Nohra Mateus-Pinilla, Richard E. Warner, and Edward J. Heske. "Home Range, Habitat Use, and Activity Patterns of Free-Roaming Domestic Cats." *Journal of Wildlife Management* 75, no. 5 (2011): 1177–1185. https:// doi.org/10.1002/jwmg.145.

Loyd, Kerrie Anne T., Sonia M. Hernandez, John P. Carroll, Kyler J. Abernathy, and Greg J. Marshall. "Quantifying Free-Roaming Domestic Cat Predation Using Animal-Borne Video Cameras." *Biological Conservation* 160 (2013): 183–189. https://doi.org/10.1016/j.biocon.2013.01.008.

Willson, S. K., I. A. Okunlola, and J. A. Novak. "Birds Be Safe: Can a Novel Cat Collar Reduce Avian Mortality by Domestic Cats (*Felis catus*)?" *Global Ecology and Conservation* 3 (2015): 359–366. https://doi.org/10.1016/j.gecco .2015.01.004.

Woods, Michael, Robbie A. McDonald, and Stephen Harris. "Predation of Wildlife by Domestic Cats *Felis catus* in Great Britain." *Mammal Review* 33, no. 2 (2003): 174–188. https://doi.org/10.1046/j.1365-2907.2003.00017.x.

## Unleash Your Cat's Inner Lion

Delgado, Mikel M., Brandon Sang Gyu Han, and Melissa J. Bain. "Domestic Cats (*Felis catus*) Prefer Freely Available Food over Food That Requires Effort." *Animal Cognition* 25 (2021): 95–102. https://doi.org/10.1007/s10071-021-01530-3.

## Blink to Me, My Love

Humphrey, Tasmin, Leanne Proops, Jemma Forman, Rebecca Spooner, and Karen McComb. "The Role of Cat Eye Narrowing Movements in Cat–Human Communication." *Scientific Reports* 10, article no. 16503 (2020). https://doi.org/10.1038/s41598-020-73426-0.

Turner, Dennis C., Gerulf Rieger, and Lorenz Gygax. "Spouses and Cats and Their Effects on Human Mood." *Anthrozoös* 16, no. 3 (2003): 213–228. https://doi.org/10.2752/089279303786992143.

## Catnip and the Cosmic Kitty

Hill, J. O., E. J. Pavlik, G. L. Smith III, G. M. Burghardt, and P. B. Coulson. "Species-Characteristic Responses to Catnip by Undomesticated Felids." *Journal of Chemical Ecology* 2 (1976): 239–253. https://doi.org/10.1007/BF00987747.

Todd, Neil B. "Inheritance of the Catnip Response in Domestic Cats." *Journal of Heredity* 53, no. 2 (1962): 54–56. https://doi.org/10.1093/oxfordjournals.jhered.a107121.

Uenoyama, Reiko, Tamako Miyazaki, Jane L. Hurst, et al. "The Characteristic Response of Domestic Cats to Plant Iridoids Allows Them to Gain Chemical Defense against Mosquitoes." *Science Advances* 7, no. 4 (2021). https://doi.org/10.1126/sciadv.abd9135.

## The Love Loop

Nagasawa, Miho, Takefumi Kikusui, Tatsushi Onaka, and Mitsuaki Ohta. "Dog's Gaze at Its Owner Increases Owner's Urinary Oxytocin during Social

Interaction." *Hormones and Behavior* 55, no. 3 (2009): 434–441. https://doi
.org/10.1016/j.yhbeh.2008.12.002.

Nissen, Eva, Gunilla Lilja, Ann-Marie Widström, and Kerstin Uvnás-Moberg.
"Elevation of Oxytocin Levels Early Post Partum in Women." *Acta Obstetricia
et Gynecologica Scandinavica* 74, no. 7 (1995): 530–533. https://doi.org/10
.3109/00016349509024384.

Reevy, Gretchen M., and Mikel M. Delgado. "Are Emotionally Attached
Companion Animal Caregivers Conscientious and Neurotic? Factors That
Affect the Human–Companion Animal Relationship." *Journal of Applied
Animal Welfare Science* 18, no. 3 (2015): 239–258. https://doi.org/10.1080
/10888705.2014.988333.

Saunders, Jessica, Layla Parast, Susan H. Babey, and Jeremy V. Miles.
"Exploring the Differences between Pet and Non-Pet Owners: Implications
for Human-Animal Interaction Research and Policy. *PLOS ONE* 12, no. 6
(2017): e0179494. https://doi.org/10.1371/journal.pone.0179494.

# Part III: The Aviary

## This Flock's Got Talent

Eda-Fujiwara, Hiroko, Aya Kanesada, Yasuharu Okamoto, Ryohei Satoh, Aiko
Watanabe, and Takenori Miyamoto. "Long-Term Maintenance and Eventual
Extinction of Preference for a Mate's Call in the Female Budgerigar." *Animal
Behaviour* 82, no. 5 (2011): 971–979. https://doi.org/10.1016/j.anbehav.2011
.07.030.

Hile, Arla G., Nancy Tyler Burley, Carol B. Coopersmith, Valerie S. Foster,
and Georg F. Striedter. "Effects of Male Vocal Learning on Female Behavior
in the Budgerigar, *Melopsittacus undulatus*." *Ethology* 111, no. 10 (2005):
901–923. https://doi.org/10.1111/j.1439-0310.2005.01105.x.

## The Secret to a Long, Happy (Bird) Marriage

Spoon, Tracey R., James R. Millam, and Donald H. Owings. "The Importance
of Mate Behavioural Compatibility in Parenting and Reproductive Success
by Cockatiels, *Nymphicus hollandicus*." *Animal Behaviour* 71, no. 2 (2006):
315–326. https://doi.org/10.1016/j.anbehav.2005.03.034.

### The Man Who Says It's Okay to Be Birdbrained

Leclercq, Sophie, Firoz M. Mian, Andrew M. Stanisz, et al. "Low-Dose Penicillin in Early Life Induces Long-Term Changes in Murine Gut Microbiota,
Brain Cytokines and Behavior." *Nature Communications* 8, article no. 15062
(2017). https://doi.org/10.1038/ncomms15062.

Rouse, Melvin L., and Kavanaugh Kaji. "Perinatal Exposure to Antibiotics
Reduces Affiliative Behavior after Post-Weaning in Zebra Finches (*Taeniopygia
guttata*)." *Behavioural Processes* 192 (2021). https://doi.org/10.1016/j.beproc
.2021.104491.

### The Messy Eaters for the Betterment of the World Society

Sebastián-González, Esther, Fernando Hiraldo, Guillermo Blanco, et al. "The
Extent, Frequency and Ecological Functions of Food Wasting by Parrots."
*Scientific Reports* 9, article no. 15280 (2019). https://doi.org/10.1038
/s41598-019-51430-3.

### The Canary's Invisible Force Field

Bale, Natalie M., Ariel E. Leon, and Dana M. Hawley. "Differential House
Finch Leukocyte Profiles during Experimental Infection with *Mycoplasma
gallisepticum* Isolates of Varying Virulence." *Avian Pathology* 49, no. 4
(2020): 342–354. https://doi.org/10.1080/03079457.2020.1753652.

Love, Ashley C., Kevin Grisham, Jeffrey B. Krall, Christopher G. Goodchild,
and Sarah E. DuRant. "Perception of Infection: Disease-Related Social Cues
Influence Immunity in Songbirds. *Biology Letters* 17, no. 6 (2021). http://doi
.org/10.1098/rsbl.2021.0125.

## Part IV: The Fish Tank

### The Guppy's Eeeeeeeevil Eye

Godin, Jean-Guy J., and Scott A. Davis. "Who Dares, Benefits: Predator
Approach Behaviour in the Guppy (*Poecilia reticulata*) Deters Predator
Pursuit." *Proceedings of the Royal Society B* 259, no. 1355 (1995): 193–200.
https://doi.org/10.1098/rspb.1995.0028.

Heathcote, Robert J. P., Jolyon Troscianko, Safi K. Darden, et al. "A Matador-Like Predator Diversion Strategy Driven by Conspicuous Coloration in Guppies." *Current Biology* 30, no. 14 (2020): 2844–2851. https://doi.org/10.1016/j.cub.2020.05.017.

## Oh, Beautiful Nanny Barbarian!

Alyan, Sofyan. "Male *Betta splendens* Are Equally Aggressive toward Neighbors and Strangers." *Journal of Ichthyology* 50 (2010): 1066–1069. https://doi.org/10.1134/S0032945210110123.

Bronstein, Paul M. "Commitments to Aggression and Nest Sites in Male *Betta splendens*." *Journal of Comparative and Physiological Psychology* 95, no. 3 (1981): 436–449. https://doi.org/10.1037/h0077780.

Johnson, Steven D. "Carrion Flowers." *Current Biology* 26, no. 13 (2016): R543–R576. https://doi.org/10.1016/j.cub.2015.07.047.

Kwon, Young Mi, Nathan Vranken, Carla Hoge, et al. "Genomic Consequences of Domestication of the Siamese Fighting Fish." *bioRxiv* (2021). https://doi.org/10.1101/2021.04.29.442030.

Rhoad, Karen D., James W. Kalat, and Peter H. Klopfer. "Aggression and Avoidance by *Betta splendens* toward Natural and Artificial Stimuli." *Animal Learning & Behavior* 3 (1975): 271–276. https://doi.org/10.3758/BF03213443.

## Your Goldfish Is Watching You

Beatty, Stephen J., Mark G. Allen, Jeff M. Whitty, et al. "First Evidence of Spawning Migration by Goldfish (*Carassius auratus*); Implications for Control of a Globally Invasive Species." *Ecology of Freshwater Fish* 26, no. 3 (2017): 444–455. https://doi.org/10.1111/eff.12288.

Brown, Culum, David Wolfenden, and Lynne Sneddon. "Goldfish (*Carassius auratus*)." In *Companion Animal Care and Welfare*, edited by James Yeates, 467–478. Hoboken, NJ: John Wiley & Sons, 2018. https://doi.org/10.1002/9781119333708.ch23.

Gee, Philip, David Stephenson, and Donald E. Wright. "Temporal Discrimination Learning of Operant Feeding in Goldfish (*Carassius auratus*)." *Journal of the Experimental Analysis of Behavior* 62, no. 1 (1994): 1–13. https://doi.org/10.1901/jeab.1994.62-1.

Lorenzoni, M., R. Dolciami, L. Ghetti, G. Pedicillo, and A. Carosi. "Fishery Biology of the Goldfish *Carassius auratus* (Linnaeus, 1758) in Lake Trasimeno (Umbria, Italy)." *Knowledge & Management of Aquatic Ecosystems* 396, article no. 1 (2010). https://doi.org/10.1051/kmae/20010001.

Lorenzoni, Massimo, Massimiliano Corboli, Lucia Ghetti, Giovanni Pedicillo, and Antonella Carosi. "Growth and Reproduction of the Goldfish *Carassius auratus*: A Case Study from Italy." In *Biological Invaders in Inland Waters: Profiles, Distribution, and Threats*, edited by Francesca Gherardi, 259–273. Dordrecht, Netherlands: Springer, 2007. https://doi.org/10.1007/978-1-4020-6029-8_13.

## Tetras Will Take You to School

Ikeda, Takehide, and Shiro Kohshima. "Why Is the Neon Tetra So Bright? Coloration for Mirror-Image Projection to Confuse Predators? 'Mirror-Image Decoy' Hypothesis." *Environmental Biology of Fishes* 86 (2009): 427–441. https://doi.org/10.1007/s10641-009-9543-y.

Lythgoe, John N., and Julia Shand. "Diel Colour Changes in the Neon Tetra *Paracheirodon innesi*." *Environmental Biology of Fishes* 8 (1983): 249–254. https://doi.org/10.1007/BF00001090.

Romano, Donato, and Cesare Stefanini. "Individual Neon Tetras (*Paracheirodon innesi*, Myers) Optimise Their Position in the Group Depending on External Selective Contexts: Lesson Learned from a Fish-Robot Hybrid School." *Biosystems Engineering* 204 (2021): 170–180. https://doi.org/10.1016/j.biosystemseng.2021.01.021.

———. "Unveiling Social Distancing Mechanisms via a Fish-Robot Hybrid Interaction." *Biological Cybernetics* 115 (2021): 565–573. https://doi.org/10.1007/s00422-021-00867-9.

# Part V: The Cage

## The Most Lovably Fierce Stink Wars

Ferris, Craig F., John F. Axelson, Lynn H. Shinto, and H. Elliott Albers. "Scent Marking and the Maintenance of Dominant/Subordinate Status in Male

Golden Hamsters." *Physiology & Behavior* 40, no. 5 (1987): 661–664. https://doi.org/10.1016/0031-9384(87)90114-4.

Huck, U. William, Robert D. Lisk, and Andrea C. Gore. "Scent Marking and Mate Choice in the Golden Hamster." *Physiology & Behavior* 35, no. 3 (1985): 389–393. https://doi.org/10.1016/0031-9384(85)90314-2.

Johnston, Robert E., Grace Chiang, and Candice Tung. "The Information in Scent Over-Marks of Golden Hamsters." *Animal Behaviour* 48, no. 2 (1994): 323–330. https://doi.org/10.1006/anbe.1994.1245.

## Home Sweet Home—Can You Dig It?

Ågren, G., Q. Zhou, and W. Zhong. "Ecology and Social Behaviour of Mongolian Gerbils, *Meriones unguiculatus*, at Xilinhot, Inner Mongolia, China." *Animal Behaviour* 37, part 1 (1989): 11–27. https://doi.org/10.1016/0003-3472(89)90002-X.

Waiblinger, Eva, and Barbara König. "Refinement of Gerbil Housing and Husbandry in the Laboratory." *Alternatives to Laboratory Animals* 32, suppl. 1 (2004): 163–169. https://doi.org/10.1177/026119290403201s27.

Wiedenmayer, Christoph. "Causation of the Ontogenetic Development of Stereotypic Digging in Gerbils." *Animal Behaviour* 53, no. 3 (1997): 461–470. https://doi.org/10.1006/anbe.1996.0296.

## Rise of the Adorable Poop Eaters

Hargaden, Maureen, and Laura Singer. "Anatomy, Physiology, and Behavior." In *The Laboratory Rabbit, Guinea Pig, Hamster, and Other Rodents*, edited by Mark A. Suckow, Karla A. Stevens, and Ronald P. Wilson, 575–602. London: Academic Press, 2012. https://doi.org/10.1016/B978-0-12-380920-9.00020-1.

Irlbeck, N. A. "How to Feed the Rabbit (*Oryctolagus cuniculus*) Gastrointestinal Tract." *Journal of Animal Science* 79, suppl. E (2001): E343–E346. https://doi.org/10.2527/jas2001.79E-SupplE343x.

Jenkins, Jeffrey R. "Feeding Recommendations for the House Rabbit." *Veterinary Clinics of North America: Exotic Animal Practice* 2, no. 1 (1999): 143–151. https://doi.org/10.1016/S1094-9194(17)30144-5.

## A Brief History of a Little Thief

Faure, Eric, and Andrew C. Kitchener. "An Archaeological and Historical Review of the Relationships between Felids and People." *Anthrozoös* 22, no. 3 (2009): 221–238. https://doi.org/10.2752/175303709X457577.

Thomson, Alexander P. D. "A History of the Ferret." *Journal of the History of Medicine and Allied Sciences* 6 (Autumn 1951): 471–480. https://doi.org/10 .1093/jhmas/VI.Autumn.471.

Vargas, Astrid, and Stanley H. Anderson. "Effects of Diet on Captive Black-Footed Ferret (*Mustela nigripes*) Food Preference." *Zoo Biology* 15, no. 2 (1996): 105–113. https://doi.org/10.1002/(SICI)1098-2361(1996)15:2<105:: AID-ZOO1>3.0.CO;2-F.

Wolf, Tiffany M. "Ferrets." In *Manual of Exotic Pet Practice*, edited by Mark A. Mitchell and Thomas N. Tully Jr., 345–374. St. Louis: Saunders, 2009. https://doi.org/10.1016/B978-141600119-5.50016-0.

## I Am Mouse, Hear Me Roar

Branchi, Igor, Daniela Santucci, Augusto Vitale, and Enrico Alleva. "Ultrasonic Vocalizations by Infant Laboratory Mice: A Preliminary Spectrographic Characterization under Different Conditions." *Developmental Psychobiology* 33, no. 3 (1998): 249–256. https://doi.org/10.1002/(SICI)1098-2302(199811)33: 3<249::AID-DEV5>3.0.CO;2-R.

Holy, Timothy E., and Zhongsheng Guo. "Ultrasonic Songs of Male Mice." *PLOS Biology* 3, no. 12 (2005): e386. https://doi.org/10.1371/journal.pbio .0030386.

Lahvis, G. P., E. Alleva, and M. L. Scattoni. "Translating Mouse Vocalizations: Prosody and Frequency Modulation." *Genes, Brain and Behavior* 10, no. 1 (2011): 4–16. https://doi.org/10.1111/j.1601-183X.2010.00603.x.

Sales, Gillian, and David Pye. *Ultrasonic Communication by Animals*. London: Chapman and Hall, 1974. https://doi.org/10.1007/978-94-011-6901-1.

Warren, Megan R., Morgan S. Spurrier, Eric D. Roth, and Joshua P. Neunuebel. "Sex Differences in Vocal Communication of Freely Interacting Adult Mice Depend upon Behavioral Context." *PLOS ONE* 13, no. 9 (2018): e0204527. https://doi.org/10.1371/journal.pone.0204527.

# Part VI: The Terrarium

## Butterfingers Superspy

DeGregorio, Brett A., Patrick J. Weatherhead, and Jinelle H. Sperry. "Ecology and Predation Behavior of Corn Snakes (*Pantherophis guttatus*) on Avian Nests." *Herpetological Conservation and Biology* 11, no. 1 (2016): 150–159. http://sperrylab.nres.illinois.edu/DeGregorio%20et%20al.%202016_%20Corn%20Snakes.pdf.

Kravchuk, Lindsay, and Charles M. Watson. "Corn Snakes Can Behaviorally Enhance Crypsis by Choosing Complex Backgrounds and Substrate." *Animal Behavior and Cognition* 7, no. 1 (2020): 39–48. https://doi.org/10.26451/abc.07.01.04.2020.

Penning, David A., and Stefan Cairns. "Prey-Handling Behaviors of Naïve *Pantherophis guttatus*." *Journal of Herpetology* 50, no. 2 (2016): 196–202. https://doi.org/10.1670/14-109.

Rush, Scott A., Kim Sash, John Carroll, Bill Palmer, and Aaron T. Fisk. "Feeding Ecology of the Snake Community of the Red Hills Region Relative to Management for Northern Bobwhite: Assessing the Diet of Snakes Using Stable Isotopes." *Copeia* 2014, no. 2 (2014): 288–296. https://doi.org/10.1643/CE-13-083.

## Have a Ball, Baby

Aubret, Fabien, Xavier Bonnet, Richard Shine, and Stephanie Maumelat. "Clutch Size Manipulation, Hatching Success and Offspring Phenotype in the Ball Python (*Python regius*)." *Biological Journal of the Linnean Society* 78, no. 2 (2003): 263–272. https://doi.org/10.1046/j.1095-8312.2003.00169.x.

Ellis, Tamir M., and Mark A. Chappell. "Metabolism, Temperature Relations, Maternal Behavior, and Reproductive Energetics in the Ball Python (*Python regius*)." *Journal of Comparative Physiology B* 157 (1987): 393–402. https://doi.org/10.1007/BF00693366.

Vinegar, Allen, Victor H. Hutchison, and Herndon G. Dowling. "Metabolism, Energetics, and Thermoregulation during Brooding of Snakes of the Genus *Python* (Reptilia, Boidae)." *Zoologica* 55, no. 2 (1970): 19–50. https://doi.org/10.5962/p.203244.

## You Can Change the Textbooks

Booth, Warren, and Gordon W. Schuett. "Molecular Genetic Evidence for Alternative Reproductive Strategies in North American Pitvipers (Serpentes: Viperidae): Long-Term Sperm Storage and Facultative Parthenogenesis." *Biological Journal of the Linnean Society* 104, no. 4 (2011): 934–942. https://doi.org/10.1111/j.1095-8312.2011.01782.x.

Booth, Warren, Gordon W. Schuett, Annice Ridgway, et al. "New Insights on Facultative Parthenogenesis in Pythons." *Biological Journal of the Linnean Society* 112, no. 3 (2014): 461–468. https://doi.org/10.1111/bij.12286.

Booth, Warren, Charles F. Smith, Pamela H. Eskridge, Shannon K. Hoss, Joseph R. Mendelson, and Gordon W. Schuett. "Facultative Parthenogenesis Discovered in Wild Vertebrates." *Biology Letters* 8, no. 6 (2012): 983–985. https://doi.org/10.1098/rsbl.2012.0666.

## Worst-Case Scenario: Call the Sentinels of Doom

Brown, Mark T., Matthew J. Cohen, Eliana Bardi, and Wesley W. Ingwersen. "Species Diversity in the Florida Everglades, USA: A Systems Approach to Calculating Biodiversity." *Aquatic Sciences* 68 (2006): 254–277. https://doi.org/10.1007/s00027-006-0854-1.

Dorcas, Michael E., John D. Willson, Robert N. Reed, et al. "Severe Mammal Declines Coincide with Proliferation of Invasive Burmese Pythons in Everglades National Park." *Proceedings of the National Academy of Sciences* 109, no. 7 (2012): 2418–2422. https://doi.org/10.1073/pnas.1115226109.

Dove, Carla J., Ray W. Snow, Michael R. Rochford, and Frank J. Mazzotti. "Birds Consumed by the Invasive Burmese Python (*Python molurus bivittatus*) in Everglades National Park, Florida, USA." *Wilson Journal of Ornithology* 123, no. 1 (2011): 126–131. https://doi.org/10.1676/10-092.1.

Richard, Shannon A., Eric A. Tillman, John S. Humphrey, Michael L. Avery, and M. Rockwell Parker. "Male Burmese Pythons Follow Female Scent Trails and Show Sex-Specific Behaviors." *Integrative Zoology* 14, no. 5 (2019): 460–469. https://doi.org/10.1111/1749-4877.12376.

Smith, Brian J., Michael S. Cherkiss, Kristen M. Hart, et al. "Betrayal: Radio-Tagged Burmese Pythons Reveal Locations of Conspecifics in Everglades National Park." *Biological Invasions* 18 (2016): 3239–3250. https://doi.org/10.1007/s10530-016-1211-5.

## Your Tarantula's Worst Nightmare

Cazier, Mont A., and Martin A. Mortenson. "Bionomical Observations on Tarantula-Hawks and Their Prey (Hymenoptera: Pompilidae: *Pepsis*)." *Annals of the Entomological Society of America* 57, no. 5 (1964): 533–541. https://doi.org/10.1093/aesa/57.5.533.

Rainer, Foelix, Bastian Rast, and Bruno Erb. "Palpal Urticating Hairs in the Tarantula *Ephebopus*: Fine Structure and Mechanism of Release." *Journal of Arachnology* 37, no. 3 (2009): 292–298. https://doi.org/10.1636/sh08-106.1.

Schmidt, Justin O. "Venom and the Good Life in Tarantula Hawks (Hymenoptera: Pompilidae): How to Eat, Not Be Eaten, and Live Long." *Journal of the Kansas Entomological Society* 77, no. 4 (2004): 402–413. https://doi.org/10.2317/E-39.1.

## Color Fight!

Dickerson, Ashton L., Katrina J. Rankin, Viviana Cadena, John A. Endler, and Devi Stuart-Fox. "Rapid Beard Darkening Predicts Contest Outcome, Not Copulation Success, in Bearded Dragon Lizards." *Animal Behaviour* 170 (2020): 167–176. https://doi.org/10.1016/j.anbehav.2020.10.014.

Smith, Kathleen R., Viviana Cadena, John A. Endler, et al. "Color Change for Thermoregulation versus Camouflage in Free-Ranging Lizards." *American Naturalist* 188, no. 6 (2016): 668–678. https://doi.org/10.1086/688765.

Smith, Kathleen R., Viviana Cadena, John A. Endler, Warren P. Porter, Michael R. Kearney, and Devi Stuart-Fox. "Colour Change on Different Body Regions Provides Thermal and Signalling Advantages in Bearded Dragon Lizards." *Proceedings of the Royal Society B* 283, no. 1832 (2016). http://doi.org/10.1098/rspb.2016.0626.

# Acknowledgments

Thank you, Robin Sutton Anders, for your skillful, sharp, and insightful edits. Thank you to Julia Ellis, who continues to have TWO deft eagle eyes, and to our agent, Gillian MacKenzie.

Our appreciation goes to the awesome and world-changing scientists who shared their work with us, especially Julie Hecht, Mikel Maria Delgado, Melvin Rouse, and Warren Booth.

Eleanor would like to thank Greg Rice.

Thank you also to Hilary Van Dusen, who's up for secret poop eaters and inner lions alike.